TO
FIGHT
THE
WILD

TO
FIGHT
THE
WILD

*Rod Ansell
and
Rachel Percy*

HARCOURT BRACE JOVANOVICH, PUBLISHERS

SAN DIEGO   NEW YORK   LONDON

Requests for permission to make copies of any
part of the work should be mailed to:
Permissions, Harcourt Brace Jovanovich, Publishers,
Orlando, Florida 32887.

Frontispiece photo of Rod Ansell by Jan Kenny, © Rachel Percy

The frontispiece photo and the photos preceding the text of Parts Two, Three, and
Four are from the dramatized documentary of *To Fight the Wild* by Richard Oxenburgh Productions.

Library of Congress Cataloging in Publication Data

Ansell, Rod.
   To fight the wild.

   Reprint. Originally published: Fremantle, W.A. :
Fremantle Arts Centre Press ; Woollahra, N.S.W. :
Currency Press, 1980.
   Summary: A man struggles to survive on his own in one
of the most isolated corners of Australia for two months
before he is rescued.
   1. Wilderness survival—Australia—Juvenile literature.
   2. Wilderness areas—Australia—Juvenile literature.
   [1. Wilderness survival.   2. Survival.   3. Australia]
   I. Percy, Rachel.   II. Birch, Robert, ill.   III. Title.
GV200.5.A57   1986   613.6'9   85-22023
ISBN 0-15-289068-8

Designed by G. B. D. Smith

Printed in the United States of America

First American edition 1986

B C D E

Contents

Part One THE ACCIDENT

1 *Getting Away from It All*   4
2 *The Fight Begins*   14

Part Two MAKING CAMP

1 *My First Kill*   28
2 *Taking Stock*   36
3 *Getting Organized*
4 *Hunting*   52

Part Three LEARNING HOW TO LIVE

1 *I Explore the River*   64
2 *Remembering Things Past*   75
3 *Night Solitude*   80
4 *Dawn and the Daily Round*   85
5 *Bees and Other Wildlife*   91
6 *Thoughts on the City and the Bush*   99
7 *Memories in Loneliness*   107

Part Four THE RESCUE

1 *Horse Bells*   120
2 *Making Tracks*   129
3 *Another Narrow Escape*   135
4 *The Road Home*   141

Postscript   145

Poems at beginning of Parts One, Two, Three, and Four are by Rod Ansell.

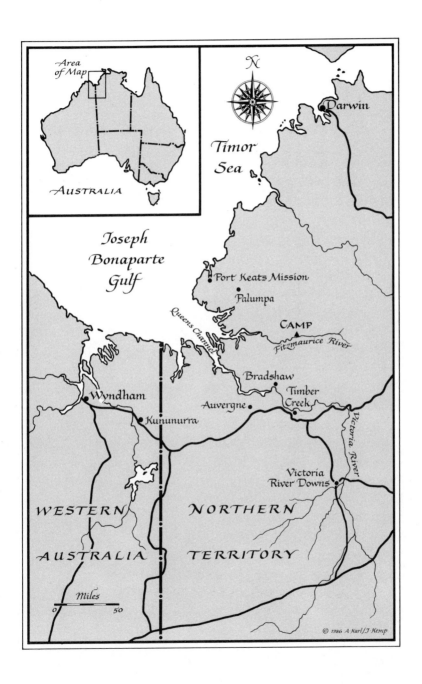

Area
of Map

AUSTRALIA

N

Timor
Sea

Darwin

Joseph
Bonaparte
Gulf

Port Keats Mission

Palumpa

CAMP

Queens Channel

Fitzmaurice River

Bradshaw

Timber
Creek

Wyndham

Auvergne

Victoria River

Kununurra

Victoria
River Downs

WESTERN

NORTHERN

AUSTRALIA

TERRITORY

Miles

0   50

© 1986 A·Karl/J·Kemp

Part One

THE ACCIDENT

Previous page: *Saltwater crocodile*
Photo by Michael Morcombe, © Richard Woldewdorp Photo Index

Dingo

Yellow dog dingo, wraith of the grass,
Melting away unnoticed you pass.
Came to the river, the vision was plain,
Quivered black nose to vanish again.

Yellow dog dingo, sorrow-full mourn,
Cry for the lost and the country unborn.
Backdrop of moon, your nose to the air,
Heart independent, our spirit you bear.

Yellow dog dingo, invisible land,
Yet countless your tracks on the ways of the sand.
Stole to the flat, gut-hung with feed,
Smiles at the wallaby too busy to heed.

How do you die where no trap is set?
Torn by the fangs of the sons you beget.
Your bones never whiten the ridges I walk,
Yet the blackboard of victims is white with their chalk.

Yellow dog dingo, invisible land,
Yet countless your tracks on the ways of the sand.
Hard is the man, by the sun he is strong,
Yet chilled is his soul when night is re-born.

Yellow dog dingo, sorrow-full mourn,
Cry for the lost and this country unborn.

1

Getting Away from It All

It was early in May. I don't know the exact date. It's a funny thing, but I just don't want to know about dates, calendars, or clocks either. Probably because none of them have much relevance to life in the bush.

I'd finished up a partial contract out from Kununurra in Western Australia and intended to go across to the Northern Territory, sort of southeast of Darwin, to see about a contract for catching buffalo. It would be a longish trip, what with the traveling and then looking into the buffalo contract pretty carefully. I hadn't caught buffalo before and wanted to check out the country and everything else thoroughly before I took it on.

Time wasn't of much importance, and I had some weeks to spare, so decided to take a couple of weeks off while I was at it. Have a holiday. Get away from it all for a spell. I'd been told that the fishing was good down the Victoria River, and I hadn't been in that area before, right down near the mouth, where it runs into the Queen's Channel. A very remote place, hardly ever visited by anyone. Untouched wilderness. That suited me. I like fishing and I like looking around—exploring new places. And I can't stand going where a mob of tourists have just been, having to trip over empty cans and all sorts of rubbish.

With the Toyota it'd be easy enough to go across country to the river, and I had two aluminum dinghies, one eighteen foot with an outboard, the other nine foot with oars, so reckoned I'd have no worries going down the river with those.

I had a couple of eight-week-old pups, bullterrier crossed with boxer, which I decided to take with me. They were getting to the age when they needed to be taught a few manners, and would be a bit of company. The parent dogs were left with Lorraine, a friend in Kununurra, who'd take good care of them, especially old Deaf Dog, who's a real dag of a dog, an old white fellow, all beaten up and as hard as nails. Deaf as a post, too, but a hell of a character. Lorraine expected me to be away about two months altogether.

Not many other people knew I was going, or if they did, for how long. They call it the land of lots of time up there, and that's how it is. Everything you do is a protracted business because it's a bit of a struggle. The country and the distances make it that way. You can't push the country, traveling off the main roads, because it won't let itself be pushed. You've got to go along with it. You can't decide that you're going to go from A to B as fast as possible because you'll probably end up with too many flat tires and there you are out in the middle of nowhere, stuck. If the roads are rough you've just got to poke along steady, look after your vehicle, and make sure you get there in one piece. It might be very annoying, very infuriating, but that's what you've got to do. If you get to a flooded creek there's no use thinking you'll dash across it or go round it. You just have to wait for it to go down, which might be two days or two weeks.

Everyone up there spends their allotted time just sitting waiting—or walking. And nobody travels any distance unless prepared for a holdup of some sort. Always have a swag (piece of waterproof canvas with blankets, tied up with a couple of straps), always have a rifle and a knife, fresh water and some tinned tucker. Everyone has the attitude that time, in the form of timetables, has nothing to do with how things happen. Besides, a bloke might say he was going to Hall's Creek to see some mates, stop at a station on the way, and get on the booze for a week. Then he might decide he doesn't want to go to bloody Hall's Creek after all and go home. Or he might end up in Darwin, because when he got to the turnoff he remembered the good time he had there last time. You might make plans but when you do you know that, one way or another, things'll probably turn out different. And if you get stuck you know you'll still get where you're going sooner or later, provided you don't lose your head and do something foolish.

From Kununurra to the Victoria was about a hundred miles, more or less, over the border into the Northern Territory. I left very early, before daylight, when it was cool and fresh, the sun just giving the tops of the ranges a red glow. Stuck to the road at first, then cut across country, taking it easy, and hit the Victoria about where the country of Auvergne and Legune Stations meet. That was only a guess as, like most of the country, it was unfenced.

Once on the river I followed it along for a couple of miles looking for a good spot to launch the boats, as the banks are very steep. A small tidal creek was suitable, where I could back up and slide the boats into position on the creek bed. Once the tide came in it was just a matter of pushing off. Most of the gear went into the eighteen-footer, with the outboard. It was quite a good little boat, but it didn't have all its flotation tanks in it. They'd been taken out when some repairs had been done and not put back in. They're that foam stuff which goes under the seats in dinghies and makes them practically unsinkable. Aluminum dinghies are hard to sink anyway, but with flotation tanks they can be pushed under, and even if full of water will bob up again to sit at water level. But I wasn't expecting any trouble. Taking the nine-footer was just a precaution in case the outboard packed up on me and I had to take to rowing.

I had a big drum of fresh water in the Toyota, so filled up a couple of four-gallon containers to take with me, as there wouldn't be any fresh water on the tidal river. There was plenty of fuel, spare parts, a toolbox (which was bolted to the bottom of the boat), plenty of ammunition and fishing gear. Not a lot of food, as I intended to catch my tucker, but there was tea, sugar, powdered milk, flour, and salt, all packed in powdered milk tins, plus a few cans of vegetables and fruit. Plenty of matches, a little gas stove and cylinder, a packet of dog biscuits for the pups. And my swag, with a rifle, knives, stone and steel and gun belt wrapped up in it, also a couple of spare shirts, a denim jacket, and jeans. I was wearing shorts, shirt, and a hat, but left my boots in the Toyota, parked in a patch of thick scrub on the riverbank. The chances of anyone seeing it, let alone stealing it, were remote. It'd be safe enough until I got back.

With everything on board, including the two puppy dogs, and towing the little boat which didn't have much in it except the oars and some odds and ends, I set off downstream.

At that point the Victoria River is about half a mile wide, salty and deep. A good, navigable river. In the early days all the supplies for stations further inland, like Victoria River Downs, used to be brought up the Victoria by boat or barge; taken upriver to a depot a hundred miles inland, where the tidal waters stopped. That was at the junction of the river and Timber Creek, which is a tributary, and the first fresh water on the river. In those days a man used to be left there full time, to guard the supplies until the stations sent their teams in to pick them up. Now it's Timber Creek township, on the highway to Darwin, but it's still not much more than a depot with a pub, a store, and a police station.

But, heading in the opposite direction, I wasn't interested in Timber Creek. With the outboard opened up and making a fair pace, I was well on my way downriver and looking forward to getting into an area I hadn't seen before. The weather was good. Typical Dry weather, clear and bright. Hot in the middle of the day, but cooler at night. Very nice conditions for a few days fishing.

By late afternoon I was down in the middle of the river where it is about two miles wide, opening out into the Channel, the banks just a blur in the distance. We were drifting, with the two pups lying quietly in the bottom of the boat, behaving themselves. Bullterriers aren't like other pups. They don't fool around much when they're little. They're very quiet and docile until they're a bit more than two months old, when they wake up and start taking an interest in things, especially in hunting cattle. I gave these two a pat and talked to them every now and again, and they were happy.

It had been a good day. I'd caught some fish and had also seen a few crocodiles, which was interesting. In fact, I was pleased with the whole area. It was what I hoped it would be. Untouched. Peaceful. Now the sun was getting right down, a big, lolly-pink ball turning the brown water into mauve and pink and a kind of gun-metal green.

The tide was about to turn. Once it did conditions would get choppy, with the outgoing tide backing up a bit against the wind that was starting to blow from the sea. It was time to run over to the shore and find a place to camp before it got too dark.

With the motor going again we were just poking along, not going real fast, not going real slow, still trailing a couple of lines. The water was very deep where I'd thrown the lines out, but the bottom there goes up and down like a yo-yo—sixty feet deep over a channel, then six feet over a mudbank—which makes it very nasty water once any kind of wind whips it up. Another good reason for getting out of it before it became rough.

I hadn't been going long when I felt a bit of a scrape and then a bump under the boat. Nothing much. Could have touched a sandbar, I thought, or a big piece of driftwood. Didn't take any notice of it.

The next thing we were up and over. Heaved right up out of the water and right over, gear and dogs flying in all directions. No warning, nothing—all I knew was that I hit the water with a hell of a splash and went down, swallowing a gutful of it on the way. When I shot to the surface I was surrounded by tins, boxes, oil-drums, every bit of gear I had. It looked like a litterbug's picnic, with the pups paddling for their lives in the middle of it.

All I could see of the big boat was the outboard sticking up out of the mess. The small dinghy was still tied to it, half swamped but afloat, and I broke all records getting to it and hardly touched the sides getting in. I had no idea what had tossed us over and I didn't want to find out. I'm touchy about salt water at the best of times—if there's one thing I'm dead-set scared of it's sharks. Not that I thought a shark had done the damage—it would have followed up and grabbed me or the pups if it had. But that water's full of them and you can't see an inch below the surface because of the muddy conditions.

The next priority was the pups. Bouncer, the brindle dog, was swimming well and soon got close enough to be dragged in, but Cindy, the little white pup, was in trouble, floundering. It did not appeal to me much, but I had to dive in and swim after her. Lifting her over into the dinghy I felt a sharp jab from bone: one hind leg was broken. Nothing to be done for her but drop her in the flooded bottom of the boat.

The big boat wasn't sinking any further, just settling into the water with the weight of the outboard keeping it down. I grabbed the towrope and tried to pull it up. Aluminum boats are light enough, but full of water and with the outboard—the rope broke. That was it. Without that "anchor" the little dinghy started to drift fast, out with the tide. So did all the gear, and with the rising wind there wasn't much hope of saving anything. Thank Christ my swag drifted close enough to be grabbed—both it and its contents were vital. I lost my water drums, which was bad, but managed to reach a tin of peas, a tin of powdered milk, another tin, a box of sodden matches, and that was all. Then it was too dark to see, with the wind blowing hard, chopping into the outgoing tide and building up very rough water.

With only one oar (I don't know what happened to the other one) I tried to steer across the current toward the nearest invisible bank. Hopeless. The waves just poured over us. I had to face into the wind to stop shipping water.

Emptying out the milk tin to use as a bailer with one hand, I fought to keep the dinghy steady into the wind with the other. Where the hell were we going? Wherever it was, out to sea or up the coast, the tide was boss. At least we were still afloat. No guarantee we'd stay that way. Sandbars and mudbanks everywhere, reefs and deep channels in between, the water going mad, whipped up by the wind and tide. A pretty desperate situation in a small boat.

Bailing, struggling with that one blasted oar, bailing, bashing through ten-foot waves, and still bailing. The spray hammering like nails. The nastiest night I've ever spent. More than that, it was a nightmare which didn't look like coming to an acceptable end.

Daylight at last. Where were we? Surrounded by an endless vista of murky gray-brown water, still fairly rough, that faded off to a hazy blue to the northwest and the open sea. The tide must have taken us quite a way out to sea and then brought us back when it turned. But not to where we'd started, because of the prevailing drift of the north. The nearest land was a long low island. I reckoned it was Quoin Island, and with the current still going in that direction I rowed with it and dragged the dinghy up onto the beach. I was really knocked up. Had to rest before anything else.

Bouncer hopped out, very pleased to be on land again. Before I could help her Cindy did the same, on three legs, the bone of the broken one sticking out through her bloody hide. Bullterriers are by nature indifferent to pain, but Cindy was extraordinarily stoical. Never complained or whimpered. Just found a dry patch of sand and lay down.

I was bone weary, exhausted. Felt as if I'd been pickled in brine, with raw eyes and salt-caked mouth. And getting bloody thirsty. It was already a lot more than twelve hours since my last drink. No good thinking about the water I'd lost. It was gone, and if the island was Quoin there was no fresh water on it either. Still, after a spell, I checked it out. Walked over its unpromising terrain, mostly just an overgrown sandbar with nothing but mangroves. No luck. We—the pups and I—were in for a long stretch without a drink.

Back at the dinghy I emptied out the rest of the water and then sat down to think things over. It was a hell of a situation. It shouldn't have happened and I was a bit nonplussed about it all. Even looking back at the accident I still didn't have much idea what had caused it. A shark or crocodile was unlikely. One of those fellows would have followed up and finished the job while we were in the water—even if one of them had been able to tip over what was a fair-sized boat. A whale was all I could think of for an explanation: maybe one had got into shallow water and panicked, coming up in a hurry right under me. I hadn't seen any signs of whales earlier, but I don't know how long they can stay under without coming up for a blow. Still, the cause was a bit beside the point. It had happened and we were in a right mess.

I was a long way from where I'd started, right over on the other side of the Queen's Channel. Going back meant crossing the Channel again and I frankly didn't want to do it. A mean, treacherous stretch of water and still too rough for comfort. Even if I could've got back to the Victoria River, it was still more than thirty miles to the only place I was sure there was fresh water: where I'd left the vehicle. Legune Station has country on the far side of the Vic, but I don't know Legune, have never worked there, and had no idea where the cattle watered. Certainly not on the river—too salty—and probably not too near it either. The homestead is a long way inland and just one spot in a wilderness. Even if I'd known where it was in relation to the river or anything else, it would be easy to miss by miles. To strike out without knowing where I was going, on the off chance, would be foolhardy in the extreme.

No. Going back was out of the question. Especially crossing that open stretch of water again. I reckoned about eighteen miles of it. They might call it the Queen's *Channel*, but eighteen miles of open water is out to sea in my opinion and I'm no seaman. Once was enough.

All the country to the east and north of there is full of rough ranges beyond the tidal salt flats. No good trying to cross any of that in a hurry. And I had no illusions about being rescued. No one would be looking for me and no one was likely to be in the area. My only faint hope was that a light aircraft might pass over on its way from Kununurra or Wyndham to Darwin or Port Keats. That wasn't really on the cards. Port Keats? I didn't even consider trying to get there. Again, I had only a

vague idea where or what it is—a mission settlement somewhere up the coast, at least a hundred miles away.

But I had no intention of just lying down to die. I had to
do something. From what I could see of the coast I reckoned
the Fitzmaurice River was fairly close. There was a narrow
channel, sheltered by a couple more islands, between me and
what looked like an estuary or inlet on the coast. I banked on
that being the Keyling Inlet, and that somewhere up it—how
far I wasn't sure—would be the mouth of the Fitzmaurice.

It is a river no one knows very much about—I certainly
didn't—except that it's totally uninhabited and runs through
deserted country. No roads approach it, no one lives within
miles of it. No stations, no Aboriginal communities. Nothing.

What I did know was that it is shorter and narrower than
the Victoria, and that therefore it was possible that the tidal
push wouldn't go as far upstream. Fresh water could be closer,
perhaps only thirty miles from the mouth. Maybe I'd get to it
in time. How long would it take? Two days, or more? I didn't
know, but could see no choice.

However, I had to wait for the next incoming tide. I needed
it to help me on my way. There was that one miserable tin of
peas. I hacked it open with a knife, drank the fluid and ate the
peas, shuddering. If there's one thing in the world I can't stand
it's cold tinned peas. The only other food I had was the second milk tin half full of sugar. I couldn't touch that. Sugar
when you're thirsty is bad news.

Then I rested, keeping one eye open for the first sign of the
incoming tide.

2

The Fight Begins

The Queen's Channel and Keyling Inlet. Best seen from the air. Looking down on it spread out below. An endless feud between land and sea. One where the boundaries of conquest shift with every tide. Where the sea devours endless miles of salt flats, swallowing up their glittering, crusted surfaces and the black slime below, until the murky water is lapping the feet of barren red hills. Where, in turn, countless tons of mud and silt invade the sea, choke it: then move and merge. The barriers forever shifting.

A wasteland. Yet from above, from afar, it is beautiful. A world washed over in palest grays, limpid greens, and the softest shades of blue, gently shining with a silver light. All traced with a series of elegant, lucid patterns. The classic patterns of arteries and veins, of leaves and trees and all living things, the patterns of life. Delicately molded by receding waters over gleaming mudbanks: darker where mangroves have clenched and gripped their roots. Every incoming tide wipes the patterns out, engulfs them in an ever-recurring cycle. A world of eerie beauty. But only when seen from the air.

I made pretty good time across the narrow channel to the estuary. It was a bit rough but not too bad, keeping to deeper water and rowing hard. Once in the estuary itself it was calmer. But it was hot. Early afternoon and the sun reflecting off the sides of the aluminum dinghy—it was like being in a little solar heater. I'd lost my hat which I missed terribly. The wind filled the air with salt, but I couldn't think about that, or about how long until I got a drink. What was a bit ironic, I heard a jet plane in the distance, on the Darwin run. A booming roar, and when I looked, a glint of sun on metal, far up in the sky. Modern technology, all very nice, but no good to me at all where I was.

From what I could see it was the most disastrous looking country all along the inlet. Mangroves, salt flats, and bare red hills in the distance. It's a dead place, no life about it at all, not even many birds. The only activity was down below. Swirls and sploshings here and there as some big fish came to the surface. Everything that swims comes in with the tidal water, from big sharks to little fishes, and a few crocodiles were about, too. Got a glimpse of a couple of snouts just cruising along—the old "I'm just a log" trick. The water was the only sound, a constant undercurrent, and the dip and splash of the oar, the clunk of it hitting the sides of the boat, must've carried for miles. A silent gray place.

As I got well up the inlet it became apparent that it wasn't going to be all that straightforward. There were two or three openings, false mouths, in the ranges ahead. It was getting late and the tide had just about run its course. The sun was going down and everything was reduced to a pink and purple haze with no visibility. I was lucky enough to find a little rocky island before it got too dark, and before the tide started to drag me back again. Pulled over to that.

It was a fairly miserable camp, but at least I was able to tie the boat up to a rock, pull my swag out, and open it up. It was wet, but softer to lie on than bare rock. Once the sun went it was cold, too. I've broken a few bones, one way and another, and when it's cold they ache; there were a few extra aches from all that rowing, as well as the usual quota. A fire would have been good. And some food. And a drink. Water, tea, hot or cold . . . even lukewarm flat beer. Anything.

The pups came and slept on the swag beside me. Poor little Cindy's leg was still bleeding, with the bone still sticking out, but there was nothing to be done about it. I probably dozed off a bit, but was afraid to sleep properly in case I missed the early morning tide.

As soon as it was light enough to see, I pushed off on a tide which was well up and coming in fast, taking me toward what looked to be the river mouth straight ahead. This caused me all sorts of concern, because I was sure the river went off to the right, but could see no sign of it doing so. We were approaching where two ranges met at an angle, and there was no way of telling what they were hiding. I had to pull up for a bit, fight the tide and keep the boat in one place, while I tried to work it out. The opening ahead looked all right with a strong rush of water heading for it. Or was the main current veering to the right? If so, into what? It took me about a quarter of an hour to make up my mind, to decide that the opening ahead was a trap, a false mouth. I went to the right, and hoped to hell it wouldn't turn out to be a fatal decision. At first I wasn't so sure, but still kept rowing that way. Then suddenly the current grabbed hard and swept us up into a gap between the ranges. It was the river.

> Once past the mouth the course of the Fitzmaurice River cuts between rocky hills, becomes deep and narrow, locked in by dark lateral cliffs that seem about to slide into the fast flowing water. Layer upon layer, they are like a mammoth chocolate cake that has been squashed, so that the layers have slipped forward. Little clumps of yellow spinifex grass follow the cracks

like dobs of cream. Millions of years have eroded this fantasy, so that the top is a broken crumbling honeycomb, and, like knives slicing, gulleys slash into the sides. Trees and vines fight for light among the boulders and fallen rubble that choke the long shafts of those gulleys, and, where silt has been caught in pockets by the river's edge, mangroves cling.

The trapped tidal waters rise with an enormous rush in this section of the river, striving to get past and up where the ranges fall back and allow broad reaches and the overflow escape of salt pans. Wet season floods and constant tidal rushes have gouged out a river that is picturesque. And treacherous.

Once in the narrow section it was a real fast toboggan ride. That gorge is as if someone had taken a monstrous great shovel and scooped a trench through the hills, and with the big tides the water is forced to rise at a terrific rate, sometimes going up over forty feet. Very fast and furious, but I still kept rowing, to keep the boat steady and stay with the main rush of the water. Every yard it took us meant we were closer to fresh water. The dogs lay low in the bottom of the boat. It wasn't a smooth ride, with all sorts of eddies and bits of whirlpools caused by changes in the river bottom and by the conflicting current still coming downstream. Driftwood was a hazard too— there were big lumps of it tumbling upstream, trees that had been uprooted in the last Wet's floods, and had been going up and down ever since.

When the run stopped, it was a bit of a business finding somewhere to tie up, the banks are so steep. I couldn't get out, had to stay in the boat and try to keep awake. As the water level fell the rope had to be let out or we would have ended up dangling upside down.

I missed part of the next tide. I don't know what happened. Must have dozed off a bit in the end. I was getting pretty thirsty by then. When I did get going I found the river widening a bit, and the water wasn't as fast. Crocodiles were following the boat. They'd float up out of their hidey-holes on the bank with the rising water, and then drift along behind us. I had the rifle out of the swag, loaded, and thought that if one came too close I'd blow him out. One did get to about ten yards off the bow and I took a shot at him. Don't know if I hit him or not, but he disappeared.

Normally a croc wouldn't be so cheeky, but those Fitz-maurice fellows have been left alone so long they don't know what it is to be scared of anything. They don't think man equals gun equals danger, and there were the two dogs in the boat, and the smell of blood from Cindy's broken leg. Crocodiles love dog better than anything. So they just floated along behind us. Must have thought it was Christmas. Shooting wouldn't have made much difference because they're territorial, and as one dropped behind there was another waiting to take its place.

I was getting more and more dehydrated. There was no doubt about that. Starting to drift a bit, mentally, sort of float away from myself. But my body kept on rowing. I was pleased with that, with the way my body just kept on going.

Time and distance didn't have much reality, but it must have been toward late afternoon when I found we were in an enor-mously broad section of water. Couldn't really tell how wide it was—could've been a mile—spreading out into salt flats on the south side where the ranges had dropped away. On the north side the hills seemed to have angled off for some dis-tance, and a big dirty-looking creek ran in to join the river.

I couldn't make up my mind about that dirty-water creek. There could have been a spring somewhere further up it, back in the hills. Sometimes you can get to fresh water quicker away from the main rivers by following one of the tributaries, but you've got to know them individually to be certain. If I was lucky I might find fresh water in a few hours. If not, if it ran back into salt pans, I'd be cactus. I'd never make up the lost time.

Another thing. There was a very big, nasty-looking whirlpool right across the mouth of that creek. Get caught in that and I'd be stuck, could go round and round like a mouse in a cage for hours.

The creek was too risky. I went on up the main stream of the river. By now it was late afternoon, the sun getting low behind the hills and visibility not too good for any distance, but I kept on rowing. While the tide kept going so would I, just automatically rowing.

It got just on dark, the stage where you can see but you can't. The river seemed to be closing in again, funneling down toward something which stood out white against the darkness. And there was a sound—a roar—which built up as I got closer, and then I realized that there was a barrier ahead, a blockage or wall of some sort, with white water raging over it.

I couldn't see what was going on, and had to wait for daylight to tackle it. I pulled out of the main current and worked over to the bank, found a sandstone shelf and tied the boat to a tree root. I stayed in the boat. Maybe I could have found somewhere to put my swag if I'd looked, but it was too dark and I was too tired—buggered. Badly dehydrated after cooking for a second day in the sun.

The pups drank some of the water but it made them sick. It was still very salty, but I thought straining it might do something. My denim jacket was a heavy one, so I dragged it out of the swag, folded it and tried pouring water through it, dripping it through into the milk tin. Useless. One taste and I chucked it away, spitting the stinging salt out, and then curled up on the swag with the dogs and just waited for daylight.

I think I was getting into a pretty delirious stage and don't remember much about it. Not clearly. I was forgetting where

I was, thinking about the past, things I'd done, people I'd
known, about home and my family, and then not knowing what
was real and what wasn't. All muddled up, but dead-set worried I'd sleep again and miss part of the next tide. On a long
night like that it was only the cold air rising off the river and
the roar of the water coming back over the barrier ahead that
kept me awake, at least part of the time. The only real consciousness was riveted on the one thing: water, fresh water,
and staying alive long enough to reach it. I wasn't going to snap
my hobbles while there was still the faintest chance. Just had
to hang on to that.

It was still very dark when the tide started its incoming run,
but while it was still just gray daylight on the water I could
see what caused the blockage. Two huge boulders ran out into
the river like a wall, jutting right out from where the hills met
again and pinched the course of the river in like an hourglass.

I moved off and approached cautiously. I didn't like the look
of it one bit. Those boulders, red granite, were about thirty
feet above the low-water line, and had only a gap of three feet
or so between them. The water was rushing around all along
the barrier and then forcing itself through the gap like an express train. There was no way I could get the boat through
and had to wait until there was just enough water to get over
the top. I couldn't wait for the safest period, those few min-
utes between changes of tide when the water holds still, because then I would have lost the tide. Would have had to wait
at least six hours for the next incoming one to take me on. That
was too long. Every hour meant the difference between living
and dying. It had got down to that.

As the tide built up so did a big whirlpool at the foot of the
bar, a nasty bit of gear strong enough, I reckoned, to pull the
boat under if we got sucked into it. At one point I found myself getting into the slack water at the edge of the whirlpool,

and was fighting hard to get out of that slack, stop us from being drawn over to the center, and get out into the main current again. As soon as there was enough water over the top of the boulders I went with it. There were about a hundred yards of rough white water ahead, and I had to try and keep to the fastest sections of smoother water because that signified a bit of depth. A lot safer than the turbulent water where a lot of boiling and bubbling meant rock not far below. It was still a rough ride, though, and I couldn't be sure I wasn't going to hit a rock and would have been in a lot of trouble if I had. The force of the current would have tipped the boat over. If that had happened I might have got out myself, swum out, but I would have lost the boat for sure, and the swag and rifle, all the basic things for survival. The dogs too. And maybe I wouldn't have made it. I don't know how deep the riverbed is there; it could have been sixty feet in that narrow pass. It was a hectic hundred yards, all noise and spray, and then we were through.

The water became fairly smooth soon after that, but it was still fast, with the river spreading out again after that tight squeeze over the boulders. I kept to the main current and battled on. That's all it was. Just a battle. I had no thought of giving up—there was always the hope of fresh water a little further on—but then, it really wasn't me rowing. It was my hands, by themselves. I took an enormous interest in those hands: they had no connection with me. They were just hands. Rowing. I was apart from my body, separated, and watching it work. That body wasn't going to give in—a kind of justification for the way it had always been pushed to its limits. But something was saying "maybe you've made a boo-boo, that you'll die, do a perish, which is a pity, a bit of a shame, really." But the hands kept rowing, with big black blood blisters all over them, which somehow didn't hurt.

Cockatoos screeched overhead. Always cockatoos along riverbanks, freshwater rivers. We were getting closer. But the sun got hotter and hotter. The dogs lay quietly, eyes closed, patient, uncomplaining, Cindy's leg with the dead and dying flesh around the broken bone.

The river narrowed again, starting to take big looping bends through flatter country. And then there was another blockage across its course. A set of low falls, stretching right across the river in a series of rocky ledges, with water pouring over them, still coming downstream. Sparkling, clear water, but not fresh. Still brackish. But it meant that fresh water was very near.

I didn't have the strength to drag the boat over the crossing, and waited again for the tide to carry me over. When it covered the rocks, I just drifted across. The upward push of the water must have been stopped to some degree by those falls, leaving just enough current to carry the boat slowly forward. We went on—drifting, rowing, how much of which I don't know.

That last section is pretty much of a haze. I was really delirious, didn't know if the boat was going forward or back. Very near to dying. The dogs started whining and sniffing the air. They could smell the good water ahead. And then the boat had drifted into the bank and stopped. Bouncer was out at once and started drinking like mad, with Cindy struggling to follow him. Fresh water at last. Not perfect, but safe. I fell out after the dogs and wallowed in the water, gulping it down, mud and all. Tried not to drink too much, not to get sick. Then lay in it and let it just soak in.

After a bit I rowed a little further upriver looking for a place to camp. I could see a grassy bank with some big trees on it ahead, and I had to have shade and somewhere to beach the boat. Those last few yards were a final effort before letting go. Once I stopped I didn't think I could start again. Now all I wanted was a long, long sleep. Being hungry again would come later.

The grassy bank had little indentations like miniature bays in it, so I could wedge the boat up into a fairly safe position. Then I hauled the swag out and dragged that up to the higher top bank. Two big trees there, wild figs, were a bit too close to the river for comfort. A third a few yards away was safer. A big shady tree with spreading branches. But if it had been a little tree I would still have dropped my swag under it. I couldn't go any further. Then I went back to get the rifle and the pups, who were having another drink and a splash.

On the way down the top bank I noticed a big croc cruising along just upriver. I kept an eye on it, but didn't really expect any trouble. But just as I got to the boat, it came straight in at the dogs. Took no notice of me, but just came in, broad daylight and all. I snatched up the rifle and blasted her. Blew her out. It was a female, with the long narrow snout, and the dogs must have been too much of a temptation for her. I knew I'd have to watch the pups real well all the time, keep them away from the river or they'd be gone for sure.

I took them with me up to the tree and started to spread the swag out, thinking I ought to try and get the blankets dry, but it was a case of good intentions. I crashed. With the pups with me on the wet swag I slept right through until next morning. If any wandering crocs had come poking about that far from the water it would have been too bad. I was too tired to care. Probably, after three nights and nearly three days without a drink, I should have been dead. Already up there in that great big bull catcher's camp in the sky. But I wasn't and that was what mattered.

Part Two

MAKING CAMP

Previous page: *Tree Rod used to mark off days*
Photo by Jan Kenny, © Rachel Percy

Bull Catcher's Song

Bull catcher turns in a cloud of dust
And the engine roars as the big bull busts
Away, muscles bulge in thick red hide,
Bull's head goes down as he hits his stride.

The trees flash by in a blur of green
And half the dangers never seen.
Now spin him tight on the open ground,
The push bar bites and a bull is down.

This man is quick with his strap in hand
And the bull kicks hard in his fight to stand
But there's an old white dog with his teeth in deep
And his legs are tied in the silent heat.

Pickup truck is parked near by
With its heavy crate and hinged bull slide.
The rope pulls tight like a well-strung bow,
Toyota spins as up he goes.

With his legs untied he stands again
To glare from his prison to the silent plain
And he hooks at the side with his curve of horn
But the boards bounce back at his strength with scorn.

Well, the work is hard for a lonely man
And the bull ends up in a labeled can
But he's too set in his ways to change
So there'll be a lot more caught on the Bulls Head Plain.

1

My First Kill

Some fifty river-miles inland the Fitzmaurice takes a series of giant loops, oxbows, through a bowl of fertile country bounded on the north by river terraces and hills but extending into flood plains on the south where the ranges fall back for some miles. The camp was on a peninsula formed by one of the bows, an accumulation of soft rich soil, lightly timbered. Down by the river's edge the peninsula's lower bank is undulating, covered with green short-cropped grass as neat as a landscaped lawn. The tree under which Rod slept was a wild peach, taking its name from the shape of its leaves. A large, friendly tree, with a colony of mourning doves in its branches. Little birds of soft pearly gray, their call is a slightly wistful note, bell-like and gently repetitive.

When I woke up late the next morning I could hardly move at first. Three nights and nearly three days with only uncomfortable camps in between all the rowing had caught up with me. That long sleep, stretched out on soft ground, had relaxed my muscles at last, and now they'd all seized up. Just sitting up hurt like hell. There was no doubt about the blood blisters all over my hands now, either. And my feet were soft and spongy from being in water for so long; when I tried to walk I hobbled like an old man.

It was a case of staggering down to the river. On the way down the top bank I noticed some cattle tracks, which was good. Cattle about meant I'd be all right for meat—later. I was starting to feel starving hungry but not fit enough yet to go out looking for a feed, so ate some of the sugar I still had. Checked the boat, which the tide had hardly touched. Had a good long drink, and then had to see to the injured pup.

I found a small piece of copper piping and some soft copper wire in the rubbish in the bottom of the dinghy, and after she had had a drink, took Cindy up to the camp and got to work on her leg. A lot of the skin and flesh had died and was very nasty looking. It had to be cut away with a knife, but all the salt water or salt air or whatever which had been washing over it all the time had stopped any infection. It wasn't festering. Just messy. When it was cleaned up I put the bone back in and splinted it up with the piece of piping and a stick, tore up a spare shirt and bandaged it well and tied it all firmly with the copper wire. It didn't look very flash but I reckoned it would do the job. Cindy just took it all quietly without giving any trouble. A very stoic little animal.

Just after I'd finished that particular job, I heard something coming down to the river. A cow, a big fat cow, and only fifty yards away, coming down a slight rise through the trees and tall dry grass. She had no idea I was there. I grabbed the gun, took about two paces out from the tree, and shot her. Dropped her on the spot. It was fantastic luck, her coming right into the camp like that, because I was in no fit state to go galloping over the country looking for a beast.

I snatched up a knife, tore over to her, and cut her throat. Even hungry as I was, I knew I had to bleed her if I wanted to keep the meat. It goes off quickly enough in that climate anyway, but if it's not bled you can't keep it any time at all.

When I'd done that I just ripped some of the hide off and got stuck into the meat straightaway. The pups came up and we all had a feed. It might sound a bit off-putting, raw meat like that, but if you're hungry enough you don't give it a thought.

After that I had a rest, then, feeling stronger, went back to the cow and cut off all the steaks, rumps, chucks, and fillets, took it back to the camp and hung it up in the tree. Had some more to eat, then slept.

That was about all I did for the next day as well. Just slept and ate. Getting strong again was going to take quite a long time. By the second day I decided that, although raw meat was all right and probably better for me than cooked, I preferred it cooked. The box of matches I'd saved was useless, a soggy disintegrated mess, so I had to think of something else.

I wanted a fire for several reasons, not just to cook with. It was cold at night, and besides, riverbanks are touchy places to camp on. All sorts of creepy crawlies tend to hang around rivers, and a fire is a good deterrent. I was about twenty yards from the water, and didn't really expect a crocodile to come wandering up that far, but with the smell of dog wafting on the wind you never knew. I'd got away with it for a couple of nights, but would feel better with a fire. Lastly, I wanted to be able to make a smoke signal, just in case a light aircraft came over my way, which was possible even if not highly likely.

Aborigines can start a fire in no time at all by cutting a notch in a stick of soft wood and then twirling another stick in the notch very fast, rubbing it between the palms of their hands. If you have the knack the friction soon starts a glow hot enough to light a bit of grass. But I could twirl a stick all day and all I'd do would be wear out my hands. There is a similar method, using a bow made from a stick and a strip of soft leather or greenhide, but I wasn't feeling too confident about that either. I decided to use the primer (the small detonator) out of one of the bullets. It isn't the safest method in the world. I wouldn't recommend it to kids and Boy Scouts because you could end up with a piece of metal in the face. So I was careful. Got the lead out of a bullet by easing it out in the barrel of the gun, then tipped the gunpowder onto a little heap of dry grass and leaves. A leather swag strap wrapped around the casing of the shell acted as a shield while I tapped the primer at the top, gently, with a knife which had a cross-guard on the handle. The tip of that metal guard was easy to control for balance and precision. It took a fair few taps before the primer went off with a smart bang, enough to ignite the powder below. Gunpowder only goes off with heat. With a bit of coaxing I had a fire going. I never let it go out after that and always had a couple of logs stuck in the hot ashes, just keeping it alight.

Having a big fire blazing that night was good. Sitting by it and watching a steak sizzling on the end of a stick was a distinct improvement on things.

By this time I'd cut some strips of greenhide and tied the pups up to keep them away from the river and tempting the crocs to a dog dinner. They—the pups—were tempted by the greenhide, though. Couldn't resist chewing it until a few good whacks taught them it wasn't a good idea.

I had also started cutting notches in a young tree, a soft wood a bit like a young boab next to the peach tree. A notch a day. Normally time is the last thing I'm concerned with, but I had a feeling that I'd lose all sense of days, weeks, or even months if no record was kept. Probably because there was nothing to pin time on to, no set plans or goals ahead, like having to be somewhere in five days time, or finishing up a job in six days, things like that. It was like living in a vacuum, no beginning or end to it, so I had to keep track of the days. I used two knives: I'd cut a notch with one and leave it in the tree, and the next day I'd swap them round. That way I'd know if a day had been missed. At this stage I had no actual plans at all, being still very weak. With fresh water and cattle about I was all right. That was enough.

By the end of the third day the meat supply was just about gone. I was so hungry I'd eaten just about thirty pounds of meat, with some assistance from the puppy dogs. I could hardly hope for another beast to come walking into the camp like the first fat cow. What was left of that kill was rotten, and being cleaned up by the kites, the little black kite hawks you find all over the North, and by the crows. Mobs of them came in for the feast.

The next morning I went out hunting, leaving the pups tied up in the camp with a good fire burning to discourage any visitors. The country there runs back into low undulating ridges covered with fairly tall dry grass and a good scattering of trees. A lot of those light-colored soft woods, like corkwoods, bauhinias and the usual mixture, including gums and a few boabs. A bit further on the timber got thicker, with some small scrub and pandanus palms. Birds everywhere. It is pretty country, but I wasn't very interested in the scenery. Cattle tracks took me to a well-used pad leading away from the river and into the thicker timber. After less than a mile it dropped down toward a dried-up swamp area. Just the place for cattle. When swamps dry out there's usually a flush of green grass, good feed, and some big trees meant it would be a popular campsite.

Sneaking along quietly I had an advantage being barefoot. My feet were toughening up again, and the soil is so soft it's no problem to walk on. But clothes were a nuisance. It's amazing how much noise jeans and jackets make, rustling, catching on twigs, and generally making a racket. It was the last time I'd go hunting wearing anything more than a pair of shorts.

I shot a young bull buffalo down in the dried swamp, one of the very few I saw in the area. From it I cut all the chucks, rump, fillets, ribs, and a forequarter. A lot of meat, and getting it back to the camp took a couple of trips, what with juggling the knives, stone, steel, and rifle as well.

Most of that buffalo meat, all that could be cut into the right kind of long thin strips, I cut up and hung to dry. Providing it's got no fat on it and is thin enough, meat dries quickly if it's hung so that the sun and air can get at each piece. Once it seals the flies can't get at it and after a few days it goes hard. When it's really dried out you can break it like a biscuit. It's probably got good food value as you don't cook it.

I got all the junk out of the bottom of the dinghy, of which the most useful item was the tail end of a roll of light fencing wire, some of which I made hooks out of. There were a couple of yards of polythene piping, which I hung up in another tree like a clothesline. With wire hooks on that and on branches of my peach tree I was able to hang up enough meat to make a reliable supply for emergencies. There wasn't much else of use amongst the junk. A little old wooden box had soggy cardboard in it, some string, and a few spare bullets. There was a rusty hunk of iron I'd used for an anchor. The bullets were the best find out of that lot. I had sixteen in the gun belt, one in the gun, and when I added them all up I had twenty-seven rounds. I reckoned that would last me a fairly long time, provided I looked after them.

What else did I have? The rifle, two knives, a steel and stone. The swag of blankets and tarpaulin, with two swag straps, one in two sections connected by the swivel chain from a set of hobbles. Three tins, including the empty pea tin and the one less than half full of sugar. Two shirts, one pair of shorts, jeans and a jacket. A belt. No boots or hat. I missed the hat, but reckoned I was pretty well equipped under the circumstances. A rope, that would be handy. I needed a good strong rope.

I also had the head of the crocodile I'd shot. Not exactly useful, but a good specimen as the croc had been about sixteen feet in length. I stuck it up in a tree to dry, thinking that all things considered there'd been good reason for shooting it, even if crocs are protected. I intended to keep that head, although getting it home might be another matter.

The next couple of days were mainly spent sleeping, only waking up enough to polish off what fresh meat was left from the young buffalo. My body was taking its time recovering from the river trip, especially the period of dehydration. But as soon as I could tackle it there was another hunting trip to be made.

This time I went out with only shorts on, even though it was a bit cool with an early morning wind. I got a young cow this time, and skinned her. Took the whole hide off carefully and took it back to the camp. I'd put a greenhide strap on the rifle, so it could go over my shoulder, but it was a bit hard struggling through the bush trying to carry the knives, steel and stone with nothing to put them in, especially all loaded up after a kill. I kept dropping things and was getting hot, tired and very cranky when I saw a young bull on my way back to the camp. I shot that, and then cut the scrotum off. When the testicles and everything had been taken out I dropped the knives and things into the empty pouch of the scrotum and tied it round my waist with a strip of greenhide.

Back at the camp, the pouch was packed with dry sand and hung up in the tree to dry out. And I made a greenhide rope from the cowhide, thinking that it was a good thing I'd learned some of the old bush methods from my father and uncle, who still like to make everything they can themselves. Once every cattle station made all the ropes they needed out of greenhide; now only a few do, and most just buy hemp—all right in its way, but nothing beats a three-strand greenhide for strength. Because it's a bit stiff and doesn't flop about it's also the best rope for making any kind of a lasso.

You spread the cowhide out flat, slosh a bit of water over it, and then cut a little hole in the center. Then you just go round and round cutting a long thin strip in an ever-increasing circle, until you've got enough for the length you want.

I reckoned I had enough by the time half the hide was cut away. A two-strand rope was all I needed. There were two trees the right distance apart close to the camp and the doubled-up strip stretched between them nicely. It had to be twisted, so I cut the swivel chain off the swag strap and used that at one end, and made a ring out of wire at the other. Once both ends were tied to the trees with more wire it was just a matter of using the steel stuck through the swivel to rotate it, twisting the two strands tighter and tighter together until the greenhide was stretched taut between the two trees. It would slacken off after a while, and need tightening up several times, but in the end it would be a good strong rope. It would come in handy if I sprained an ankle or broke a leg and couldn't hunt, or if I lost the gun or ran out of ammunition. I could use it to trap a beast.

2

Taking Stock

A couple of days later I went for a walk some distance up the river, checking out the area, then sat down to have a think about making some kind of plan. I had done everything I could to feel secure where I was. There was good water and cattle. I'd made dried rations, a rope, and had a fair supply of ammunition. I had a fire. I knew I could last out where I was for a long time, but had to think about what to do eventually.

From what could be seen across the river there were no cattle on the other side. The grass along the bank was very tall, six feet high in places, with no sign of having been eaten down. No breaks in the banks from stock beating a path to water. There were wild pigs over there, I'd heard them squealing, and there were dingoes and wallabies, but no cattle.

I really didn't know much about the area. On the north side the country looked pretty rough; there was a very big flat-topped hill or long high ridge which met the river opposite my camp and then flanked it going upstream. Downstream the country soon ran up to meet ranges in the distance, and so far as I knew it was empty country. I'd not heard of any stations over there,

and the lack of cattle pointed to its being no-man's-land, probably part of a huge Aboriginal reserve, I thought. Upriver was
equally unpromising. The river ran into hills again, and I did
know it was a very long way to the nearest station country.

My side of the river was a better proposition. The cattle must
have come in from somewhere, and had been there for some
time by the look of the close-cropped couch grass along the
bank and the breaks they'd made getting down to water. But
they were all cleanskins, had never been branded or handled
at all. They were to all intents and purposes wild cattle. I
reckoned they probably came from Bradshaw, which has a lot
of country on the Victoria and, for all I knew, running back
toward the Fitzmaurice. (I'd heard of Bradshaw, but that was
all. The homestead was "on the Victoria somewhere" which
could have meant it was twenty miles from the river and on
the far side. In fact, as I found out later, Bradshaw homestead
is right on the Victoria, and on the north bank. If I had known
that at the time I might have made a dash for it, although it
was still a long way to walk and the chances of hitting the
homestead were not all that great.)

Walking across country barefoot was the least of my worries. That's one thing about being a "ballbearing cowboy," for
having taken to chasing cattle in a vehicle instead of on a horse.
Sump oil and grease rots the stitching in boots and they fall
apart, so I hardly ever wore boots, anyway.

It was the old story of water, and not knowing where it was.
There were sure to be some waterholes and creeks not dried
up, but finding them was another matter. Following cattle pads
is not a sure method, often they just lead to a dried-out swamp
like the one where I'd shot the buffalo. The only place I was
certain I'd get water was Timber Creek, and that meant going
across country until I hit the Victoria and then following that
up to the junction. Well over a hundred miles by the kind of

route you have to take in rough country, because there is no
way you can walk in a straight line. The broken ranges and
massive great jump-ups (cliffs) force you to work your way
around them. A mile on the map gets multiplied by x in real
terms.

I tried to think of some way to carry enough water. It's funny,
considering the kind of country they lived in, but I don't know
of any Aboriginal tribes who had anything to carry water in.
No waterbags or such. Only little coolimon dishes, bits of
curved bark, and carrying one of those would be like taking a
can of Coke on a thousand-mile journey.

There is a way of making a waterbag out of the second
stomach of a cow, but I had no idea of the right curing pro-
cess. If it wasn't done properly it could split on you halfway
across a dry trek, which would be bad news. All I had were
the milk tins and that wouldn't be enough for me and the dogs.

And that was another thing. Cindy's leg wouldn't be healed
for some weeks, and it'd be too hard to carry her. I wouldn't
have left her, or destroyed her—there was no question of that.
She was a good little pup, had never complained with the broken leg, was very obedient, and did the right things.

I breed bullterriers as working dogs. If there's five pups and
I take them out to start training them, three may do the right
thing and get onto a bull and hang on, but two just run around
and bark. I shoot those two right away. They are of no value,
they've done the wrong thing and that's it. Whereas Cindy was
a good little pup and I certainly had no excuse—except for my
own sake—for hitting her on the head. Bullterriers are the sort
of dog that always give the complete measure when it comes
to work. With that sort of loyalty from them I can't very well
give less.

We had to wait a month at least. And after that? The longer
I left it the less chance of finding water, as the Dry continued.

Until the Wet. The first rains could come in early October. Five months. It looked like we were stuck for that time. Not lost—you can't be lost if you know where you are. Just stuck. We'd walk out when the rains came.

The one thing which really upset me about all of that was losing out on the buffalo-catching contract. Not to show up for the job at all was bad, but there wasn't much to be done about it.

The prospect of being by myself for about five months didn't unduly concern me—not then, anyway. Not at the start. I'd been alone before, plenty of times. Never, true enough, over a long period of time in a situation of absolutely no contact even if I'd wanted it. But at that stage I didn't consider that aspect. I like the bush, have always liked it, so it was going to be the sort of thing I'd done before, only for a lot longer. You couldn't say I was content to stay, but almost. Resigned to it, anyway.

The fact of being so far from any help in the case of an accident didn't enter into it that much. Most accidents out in the bush either affect you badly or not at all. If it's serious the thought that there's someone else thirty miles or so away is very little comfort at all. So unless a bloke is in the company of someone, or within calling distance, other people don't enter into it.

For example, if I was out bull catching, with a truck driver in the camp waiting for me to take him out to the bulls I'd caught, and in the meantime I rolled the catcher miles away and got pinned by it, I couldn't expect any help for a long time. The driver would wait a couple of hours after the time I'd said I'd be back before he started looking. Then he'd have to track me all over the place, because I'd have gone where the cattle went, and be doing cloverleafs all the time. Anyone tracking would come onto masses of crisscrossed tracks and have to keep

cutting very wide to pick up the direction again. Laboriously
slow work, it would probably take until the next day. If someone gets injured in the bush and can't help himself, by the time
help arrives he's most likely going to be past needing it. He'll
have snapped his hobbles and died.

The same thing applies to snakebite. A lot of people who
get bitten right out in the bush can't get to a hospital or anywhere with antivenin for six hours or more. A lethal snake kills
you quicker than that. Tourniquets might help slow things
down, but I reckon if I was bitten by a king brown out in the
bush and didn't get antivenin for six hours I'd be dead anyway, if I was going to die.

On the whole, as far as I was concerned, being out on the
Fitzmaurice alone wasn't going to be any more or less dangerous then working out in the bush anywhere. The only thing
was if I injured an eye or foot or leg, so that I couldn't hunt
properly. That was all. It's a matter of luck, really. You trip
and break your neck in a city street. If you start worrying about
that sort of thing too much then it's time to get out of the bush
altogether. I reckoned I'd be all right, so long as I didn't do
anything foolish.

I suppose I had what most people would call a pretty old-fashioned sort of upbringing, very much in the old Australian bush
tradition.

My father in his early days was a scrubber-runner and horse-
breaker, and my uncle went cattle-droving when he was sixteen. By the time he was twenty my uncle, Les Hair, was
managing Jo Jo Station, west of Springsure in central southern
Queensland. Very rugged country which had been neglected
so that the cattle had gone wild, the ranges full of cleanskins
and bulls which had never seen a man or a horse before.

My family moved out there when I was a baby; my parents,
elder brother, and two sisters, and we all lived there off and

on until I was about eleven and we moved to Murgon. Jo Jo is pretty well controlled now, still not many fences, but the scrub bulls have been thrown and castrated and nearly all branded, and the cattle have been handled and can be mustered in the normal fashion. But in the early days—say twenty years ago—they couldn't be worked like that.

Cattle are like any other animal, and if they revert to a completely wild state, bulls have no respect for a horse or a man. They will refuse to alter their course in any way and gallop straight over the top of a horse and rider. In circumstances like that they have to be thrown, off horseback. The rider gives the bull a good gallop, pushing him so that he keeps galloping but doesn't feel threatened enough to turn and charge. It's a matter of riding a fine line until the bull, being a big animal, tires and drops to a rolling canter. Then the rider steps off his horse and runs in very quickly. All the bull can hear is the horse's hoofbeats still coming, and the next thing he knows he's been grabbed by the tail and he's down. It can usually only be done once, because if you try a second time the bull's looking out of the corner of his eye as he's cantering along and waiting for you to step off your horse. Then he spins straight round and you're in a lot of trouble.

When a bull is thrown, out in the scrub like that, its legs are tied with a strap and its horns cut off close to the head. It can't be castrated then because it might have to walk a long way to the nearest yard and so get sore or infected or just very cranky about it all. The horns are cut off as a safety measure, so it can't kill the horses, then it's led up and into a mob of quiet cattle, which are called coachers. With, say, forty coachers you can handle about twenty-five bulls and then you have to take them all off to a yard somewhere and draft off your bulls. With three or four old bulls with the coachers they won't even think of looking up, but once you get too many a general sort of untamedness goes through the mob, the bulls communicating with one another until they all think they're a pretty wild mob and shoot through. Up to that point the dogs keep them in line, a team of bullterriers that jump onto any bull that tries to break out.

That was the kind of work I was brought up with. My father, uncle, and aunt all throwing bulls and the older kids handling the coachers. My aunt is the only woman I know of who could throw a full-grown bull, jump off her horse at a flat gallop, and grab him by the tail and pull him over, no worries at all. She's a big woman, over six feet tall, but she's very feminine, with long dark hair. My uncle is a very tall and strong man, but my father is like me, a little bloke, only nine stone wringing wet.

You don't have to be big to throw a bull. You have to be fit and strong, but it's not overall strength. It's timing, getting a beast off balance. A lot of times you can throw a bull without having to put much weight onto his tail at all. As he turns to hook at you from one side you just step to the other side, and he tries to spin round to that side in a hurry. Do that a couple of times and he's trying to make a big change of direction and hooking back at the same time, and he just trips himself up. It's one of those things that might sound suicidal, throwing bulls by the tail, and there's no doubt it can be dangerous, but not all that much if you know what you're doing.

Age, size, didn't make any difference on Jo Jo. There weren't many men employed, most of the work was done by the family, and although other people weren't expected to be able to throw bulls, the kids were. We were started off on small heifers, then cows and small mickeys (young bulls, not fully grown) and even after we left and went to Murgon my father carried on teaching me. He had a block out from Murgon in conjunction with Uncle Les so there was always cattle work. And horses, always horses.

I had left home and gone up North when I was about seventeen, working on Victoria River Downs. After I'd been there about a year and was out in one of the cattle camps, I met some bull catchers who had a contract with V.R.D., and that was my introduction to bull catching as it's done in the Territory and the Far North generally.

I went out with them a few times—Bull Catchers Incorporated, that was their name—and I liked the way they did it. Very efficient. Very neat and tidy. This form of bull catching is different from that which I'd grown up with, being done with vehicles. The climate is too hot in the Far North to use horses. By the time you've galloped one bull to pump him out and throw him, your horse is in a lather of sweat and distressed. Takes him an hour in the shade to cool down, whereas in southern Queensland you can gallop a fit horse all day without doing him too much damage, because it's a lot cooler. In the North it's better to use vehicles. Either tire the bulls out so you can jump out and throw them by the tail, or actually push them over with the vehicle.

After the bull is strapped its horns are tipped, not cut close as in horse work, but just tipped, and then a four-wheel-drive truck comes up and the bull is winched into it. He goes up a slide and as soon as he's in the truck the straps come off and he can stand. Ten bulls is an average load, and that's taken to a yard. Once you've got enough to fill a road-train they're sent off to the meatworks. Some go for live export.

It sounds a tough way to catch cattle, but they don't get knocked about any more than being mustered into yards, if it's done the right way. Apart from humane reasons, bruising is to be avoided because it's docked from the price at the meatworks.

There's always a lot of wild bulls even under normal conditions in the North because it's such a big country, and it's better for stations to contract catchers than to try and control the bulls themselves. The standard arrangement is fifty-fifty, half the price received going to the catcher, but sometimes he gets more. As each bull is worth a hundred dollars on average, there's a fair bit of money in it, although overheads are high. A contractor needs two four-wheel-drive vehicles, usually Toyotas, a four-wheel-drive truck, portable yards, water pump, welding equipment, and a full range of spares and repair tools; and has to pay wages to at least one other man, the truck driver. It's very hard on vehicles, but a contractor can make a lot of money if he works hard and not too many things go wrong. It's not as skilled as the old method of catching off a horse— practically anyone can do it if he's fit and prepared to work hard during seven months of the year. You can't catch during the Wet, only during the dry months.

I joined Bull Catchers Incorporated and they taught me a lot about the business, and I bought my own Toyota and started up myself. It was hard because I had to learn all about vehicles and mechanics and doing my own maintenance, having been used to horses. The catcher Toyotas have to be adapted and cut right down. No doors, no windscreen. Put on bull bars and roll bars, build up the springs fairly heavy, reinforce the chassis, shift the radiator to up behind the cab to keep it clear of damage, things like that. And then you just about write a vehicle off in one season if it gets too knocked about.

But I like the work. It's not just the prospect of making good money, it's the independence, being your own boss. And it is like being able to cheat at your favorite game. It's not as dangerous as throwing off a horse and you can get a lot more cattle in a shorter time, so it's good. I guess it's a young man's job, although there's no real age limit. I might get to be thirty and decide I've been hurt too many times, I don't know. Accidents usually only happen when you get careless.

3

Getting Organized

The next morning there was a mean wind blowing, stirring up the white cockatoos along the river, and stirring up a pack of dust. The alluvial soil just there is very fine, like talcum powder. Silky to walk on, but with me camped on the one spot all the time it had soon broken down, and the swag was full of gray dust. It looked nice up in the tree itself, just as shady as below, but no dust and no bities, either.

Snakes weren't a real worry. It was approaching their hibernation period, but I had seen one king brown near the camp. I'd grabbed a piece of wood and donged him, mainly because of the pups. They've got no brains at all when it comes to snakes. I lost a good bitch a couple of years back from snake bite. She came galloping across the flat with a bloody great king brown in her mouth. Hadn't bothered to kill it, hadn't bothered to grab it close to the head. Just had it by the middle, twisting all around her, and of course it bit her x number of times and she took no notice, being too excited and pleased with herself to feel any pain. That was the end of her.

But if snakes weren't a problem there were plenty of ants

about. Big red meat-ants. They can cause a bit of commotion
if they get in your swag. And scorpions. A lot of them in that
country. Some big ones, but more often little tiny ones. About
the length of a matchstick, that tend to hide in dark places and
do the old wander at night. Their sting is vicious. Not deadly,
at least, I think you'd have to be in a pretty crook state of health
in the first place for one to kill you, but they can make you
feel very bad and cause temporary paralysis around the area
stung. They're best avoided.

Walking out from the camp I spotted a little green bush, only
a foot or so high, with berries on it. A wild gooseberry bush.
Good. I'd missed that one when looking earlier, so the berries
went down well. They're not bad when they're ripe, wild
gooseberries, and I needed fruit to try and balance my diet.

Everyone in the bush eats a lot of meat, but even in the
roughest camp there's flour and sugar, tea and salt, beans and
a few spuds and onions. Tomato sauce, golden syrup, and
maybe tinned vegetables on special occasions. There wasn't
much bush tucker in the area around my camp, in the way of
fruit and that, and I was always on the lookout for anything
edible.

Yams are good, like starchy potatoes, and I knew there should
be some around, especially in swampy patches, but try finding
them when the plant—the little creeper—has died off. One bit
of dried foliage looks like another bit of dried foliage to me,
and the yam, the tuberous root, can be three feet under-
ground. Blackfellows can find them easy, but I only found one
or two small ones the whole time I was there. There were a
few bush nuts, like wild almonds, which haven't much in them,
but taste all right. Not many of those about, nor conkerber-
ries, which were something else I didn't mind eating. Wild figs
are sometimes fairly sweet, it depends on the type of country
the tree is on, but it was too early in the season for many of

those to be ripe. And the wild peach is just a little berry, hard and green, nothing like a real peach. Don't know if it's edible. The gooseberries were by far the best and most plentiful fruit around, but that was only by comparison to the lack of everything else.

At the rate I was going all the edible berries and nuts anywhere near the camp were going to be cleaned up pretty soon. At least I was getting them when I needed them most.

Some people reckon boab nuts are all right, and say they've got vitamin C in them. They taste like sour powdered milk to me. Aboriginal kids like them, but kids will eat anything. Personally, I'd as soon eat chalk, and doubt they've any food value. It's like the stories about boabs full of water. If you chewed the soft wood or the root of a young one you'd get some moisture, I suppose. The "bottle tree" tag is because of its shape— that bulging bulbous trunk as the tree gets older; that, and the fact that sometimes one will have split sections or be hollow, and those cavities can catch and hold water like little tanks. But I wouldn't like to gallop about the country thinking I was going to get a drink any time I wanted from every boab tree I saw.

It was still hot during the day, although the nights were getting colder, and when it's cold all the warmth goes out of your swag if you're sleeping on the ground—gets drawn out. You need as many blankets underneath as you do on top, just to keep the warmth in.

All things considered, getting the swag off the ground in some way was going to make things more comfortable. If I was going to be there for five months it was worth thinking about.

The wild peach was a big old split tree, with three main branches spreading out at ground level and dividing again further up. It would do very nicely.

Using a knife, hitting it with a flat stone, I cut notches in the tree, then wedged two long branches, morticed them in, and tied them with some wire. A lot of shorter branches were put crossways over the other two, and wired to keep them firm, making a platform. Then I just pulled up a big mob of dry grass to make a good thick padding and threw the swag up on top of the lot. Almost like home. Up there I got any breeze during the day and it was definitely warmer at night.

The next job was to start making another oar for my dinghy. I'd had quite enough of the one-oar method of rowing, and I wanted to be able to get over to the other side of the river, and also go upstream a bit and have a look about.

I cut down one of the young softwood trees, a nice straight one, using the knife again like a hand ax. It didn't take long, about an hour with a good, strong, very sharp knife. If I had to choose between being stuck in the bush without a knife or without a gun I think I'd do without the gun.

After dragging the log into camp I knocked off the thick spongy bark and then started working it into shape, using the knife like an adz and hitting it with a flat stone. It was one of those long-term jobs, to be worked at off and on over several days. I took it easy, not having too much energy to spare at that stage. Wasn't feeling too bad, but soon knocked up after doing anything strenuous. A sort of convalescent period, still getting over the effects of being so badly dehydrated.

Cindy's leg seemed to be making good progress, but she had to be kept still as much as possible. I used to give them both a spell from being tied up every day. Take them down to the river and let them have a bit of a cool-off and a play on the riverbank, keeping watch over them, with the rifle handy in case of crocodiles. Bouncer would have a good run around, but I'd keep Cindy quietly beside me until I took them back up to the camp. The dressing on her leg was getting very scungy, but I wasn't game to touch it until the bone had had time to begin setting.

I'd wait until the sun was high overhead before I went in for a wash myself. It was warmer for one thing. I'm pretty chicken about cold water; and also with the sun at a high angle you can see almost to the bottom. It's shallow for a few feet and then drops sharply away to a fair depth, really deep in the middle. A beautiful stretch of river, a hundred yards wide, clear and green, just asking to be swum in. But no way would I go swimming, although no doubt the crocs hoped I would. There hadn't been any more trouble since that first one, but there were a couple keeping an eye on us. Just a "stick" cruising past the camp every now and again, checking us out.

I was careful not to form a very set pattern of habits. Always went down to fill the dog's water tin or to get a drink, anything like that, at a slightly different time each day. Crocodiles are great on habits, especially those of future meals. One will watch something, a beast or a man, come down every day to the river at the same time for three weeks and never give a hint of intentions. On the twenty-second day he's waiting. Down comes dinner. Snap.

Being alone I was cautious. Just went in to above the knees and dippered water over myself, scooped up handfuls of wet sand and scrubbed off any caked blood or dirt, then ducked under for a quick rinse. Clothes got the same treatment. They wouldn't have passed for a Rinso ad but were freshened up a bit.

Sitting in the sun on the grassy bank to dry off after a wash was pleasant. Just sitting looking at the clean, untouched river flowing past, the big red ridge beyond: listening to the life of the bush going on all around. Birds everywhere. Big mobs of cockatoos, white corellas, and some of the larger sulphur crested ones, a few black cockatoos with red tail feathers, all very noisy, with slightly different raucous cries. Very colorful rosella parrots, finches, kingfishers, doves. All sorts, all busy, all singing and calling out. The bush is never silent. Sometimes a couple of pelicans would sail past, very dignified; small sandpipers go poking about along the water's edge, or a big black cormorant come up from diving for a fish, sticking his neck, like a snake, up out of the water, then dodging under again.

There were plenty of fish in the river, no doubt about that. I wished my lines hadn't been lost. Thought about making a hook out of some of the wire and a line from greenhide, but reckoned it was easier said than done, and the school sharks would eat the line before anything took the hook, anyway. The school sharks are genuine sharks, and go round in packs. They'd come up with the tide and didn't seem to mind the fresh quality of the water that far upriver. I don't know if they're a species on their own, or whether they're just young sharks. They look a bit like a small gray nurse and don't get much bigger than three or four feet in length, but have a nasty set of teeth— true overlocking shark-type teeth. They're not bad eating when fresh caught, although the flesh is on the soft side.

There were barramundi there too. When a big tide came in at night I used to hear them chopping as they came to the surface. In fact, a big tide made a hell of a noise at night, all sorts of splashings and swirling about. And piles of driftwood knocking together. Sometimes a really big splash as a crocodile hit the water. They used to snap too, bring their jaws together with a clap like a small rifle shot.

I knew there were bream in the river as well, and catfish and rifle fish, and if I hadn't had the gun I would have been forced into trying to catch some. Perhaps I would in the long run, when the ammunition got low. When that happened, I thought, I'd have to try and spear them in the shallows or along a bar. Like finding yams, spearing fish is something the Aborigines are very good at. Although beef is their main food these days, and a lot have lost their old skills, there are still plenty of blackfellows who are practiced at finding and catching bush tucker. A whitefellow would be hard put to catch a wild bird without a trap or a lure, but a skilled Aborigine can see one up in a tree, pick up a stick and, with a flick of the wrist, send it flying right on target. That takes strength as well as accuracy. As far as the fish went, I'd need a lot of patience before I ever got myself a fish. It was something to try if I had to.

4

Hunting

I wondered how I would have got on without the gun. Having a rifle in the first place was probably a lifesaver. I don't know how I would have got on without it when I was still very weak. It would have been very difficult to get enough food. I mightn't have made it. The pups were too young, and with one injured anyway, I might never have got close enough to a beast to pull it down and cut its throat. It is a definite possibility that I wouldn't have got through the early stages without the rifle. Even most lizards and goannas take some catching, move pretty fast. And even if I had been able to survive maybe I'd never have got strong enough to walk out. That was a thought, being there for years, a real old feller. Rip Van Winkle. But then that wouldn't happen because as soon as the pups grew full size I'd use them for hunting. Was going to have to do that anyway, sooner or later. The sooner the better. Make the ammunition last as long as possible.

Both the pups were old enough to start training, but Cindy had to wait because of her leg. I took Bouncer with me the next time I went out, keeping him on a greenhide leash. Poor old Cindy looked very down in the mouth about being left behind, didn't like it at all.

Bullterriers are natural hunters, fantastic hunting dogs. But they have to be introduced to it. Once they've got the idea and get started that's all they live for. Like old Deaf Dog. Soppiest dog alive with people—drools all over you, scratch his tummy and he's yours for life. Has practically no teeth, they've been pulled out from hanging onto bulls, has a steel pin in one shoulder, has had all his guts pushed back in and sewn up again after a bull ripped him open. Has been jumped on and kicked and generally pounded around, but show him a bull and he's flat out after it. Hard to hold back and you have to choke him off once he gets a grip. Missing teeth or not, he can still hang on and never lets go. Tries to suck them to death.

Bouncer had to learn, had to get a taste for blood and learn to run, to get hot. They're no good until they get hot, learn to run hard enough to get their blood up, get the adrenalin going, but once they're hot there's no stopping them.

I shot a wallaby, one of the agile wallabies that are thick on the river plains, and gave Bouncer his first lesson with that. Let him lick the blood, smell it, and then swung the body around to get him excited and wanting to start chasing it. That was all he needed to get him started. As soon as he showed the right kind of interest I patted him and told him what a good dog he was, and kept up that kind of pattern with any kill I made after that. Once Cindy was well enough she got introduced in the same way.

I had to start them on something small and would only put them onto old cows or small heifers, nothing too big for them, until they were older. If you start a young dog on an old bull it can get hurt or killed. They need time to learn what they can and cannot do.

That's why Deaf Dog is deaf. He'd flown into a bull when

he was only a pup, and had got jumped on, his head bashed in. If I'd had a gun with me at the time I would have shot him, he looked so bad. But I didn't have a gun, and hadn't the heart to hit him on the head, although I felt that was what I should have done. Well, he recovered but has been stone-deaf ever since. Works to sign language—except when he doesn't feel like looking.

I ate the wallaby. It made a change in diet and I could use all of it before it went off. That was the only trouble with killing a beast, the terrific amount of waste, with no way of keeping it fresh for more than a few days. It seemed a bit hard, having to waste so much of a big animal, although I've got no feelings about killing things. Fair enough, I don't believe in anyone going out and shooting anything for fun, but I don't know how many times people—town visitors and that—have said, "Oh, you've killed that poor animal," and all I've been doing is getting some meat to eat. They think it's terrible, and then go home and get a steak out of the fridge. It's just like a big-time gangster who says: "Rightyo Bugsy, go and knock that fellow over." Well, that doesn't make the gangster pure just because he didn't do it himself. If you're going to buy beef from a butcher shop, that doesn't make you an angel. It's just the same with anyone who wears leather shoes, fur coats, anything like that—you've killed animals just as effectively as if you've done it yourself; just gone at it in a roundabout way. That's all right, but don't be hypocritical about it.

People are funny about animals, got this idea that the bigger an animal is the more right it has to live. Now if a mouse runs across the floor, even the old ladies will try and hit it with a shoe, leap on it. They're going to kill it, murder it. But it's all right, it's just a mouse, same as they'd stamp on an ant or a cockroach or anything small, that's quite okay. But let it get bigger than a mouse, or say bigger than a rat, and all of a sudden it's got this tremendous right to live. Doesn't matter if it's a possum or a pussy cat or a deer or a mongrel buffalo in the Territory, for some reason it's got this tremendous right to live, simply because it's bigger. Anything small they'll kill, anything, no matter what it is, they'll kill it, and enjoy doing it, jump on it, thrash it to pieces. I can't ever work that out. Why these things have got to be a certain size before they can stay alive. It's got me beat.

Another thing I don't understand. It's all right to have big mobs of cattle, earmark them, castrate them, fatten them up. They can graze out there in the paddock for three years and then get taken to the meatworks and get killed. Now it's not nice, but it's all right because it means meat in the butcher shops. But there's three hundred thousand buffalo destroying the Northern Territory and you can't shoot one of them. That's an outrage, because they're a wild animal. Not an indigenous one; introduced (which people seem to forget) but still a wild animal. Now what gives the buffalo, who's outside the fence, more right to live than the beast who's inside the fence, who's got the worst deal anyway because he's only got three years to live? I just can't work it out.

Take donkeys. There are thousands and thousands of them running wild in the North. Doing a lot of damage to good grass country, and yet people get upset when they're shot. They're not indigenous either; they came into the country years ago when donkey teams were used, and now they've bred up into a horde. Like any feral animal, they upset the natural balance even more than domestic ones, because their numbers are uncontrolled.

I don't shoot for sport, but I've shot donkeys as a wet season job, when cattle prices were high and it paid to shoot donkeys at seven cents a pound for pet food. I didn't like it much, but it was work during the Wet when most other work has to stop.

No one likes shooting things in vast numbers. It sends you deaf amongst other things. And it's the most dirty, filthy, indescribable job you'd ever come across. A shooter goes out with one other bloke and shoots his fifteen or twenty donkeys generally by nine o'clock in the morning. Then the other bloke starts skinning and you start boning out the carcasses. Fifteen or twenty donkeys is a ton or more of meat, all of which gives you a nice blood shower as you throw it up on the Toyota, and it's stinking hot during the Wet. You drive back to camp just before sundown and get all that meat into the freezer truck and hung up. Every fortnight, when the freezer truck is full, it's all got to be taken into town and unloaded into the processing plant. And lastly it's all loaded again (boxed) into trucks to go down to Perth.

The worst part of it is it's a seven-day-a-week job with no time to wash your clothes. When the maggots start crawling out of your pockets you stick everything into a forty-four gallon drum and boil it all up, and everything comes out the same black dirty gray color. I didn't enjoy it much, but not because of feeling sentimental about the donkeys. There were four of us operating on the one station for a whole season, we must have shot thousands of them, but it didn't even make a dent in their numbers. At least the meat was going to be of some use (probably feeding an R.S.P.C.A. member's pet puppy). When cattle prices dropped so low that prime bullocks were selling for the same amount as donkey meat, then that put a stop to large-scale shooting. The donkey population has now exploded. But when prices go up again and the shooters move in someone's bound to raise an outcry.

I can't work out why it's supposed to be such a terrible thing to shoot something: "It's against nature to kill something." But everything in the natural world dies a violent death, far more painful than a bullet. A bullet's the quickest death that a wild animal could ever wish for. Apart from that it's either going to die from old age and starvation, get torn to pieces by a predator, get bogged in a water hole and drown, die in a bush fire, or suffer slow death from sickness or injury. They've got no other possibilities, and it's a pretty sad lot. People seem to devise all sorts of sudden deaths for themselves—wars, motor cars, and things like that—make it very quick. But you can't go and shoot a wallaby, that's bad.

I'd been in the camp for two weeks, marking the end of each week with a cross on the "day tree," and was at last feeling fairly fit. Cindy's leg was coming on too, and I reckoned I could risk taking the dressing off, to check the break and clean things up a bit. Took everything off carefully, then put Cindy up on the swag and told her to keep quiet while I took the bandages and splint down to the river and washed them as best I could without soap. They were pretty filthy, but at least the clean water got rid of some of the stink. While everything was drying I sat with Cindy to keep her still. Talked to her, while she grinned at me in her amiable bullterrier way. They're such lazy, good-natured fools of dogs it's hard to imagine what they can do to a bull—or to another dog in a fight, for that matter. I wouldn't say they go looking for fights as a rule, but they don't turn one down if it's pushed on them, either.

I'm a bit the same, I suppose. I don't look for a fight, but I can't see the sense in arguing about something. A couple of blokes standing yelling "You're wrong, I'm right" at each other doesn't make any sense at all. In that kind of situation I'd as soon walk away. The trouble is, if you do that, the other bloke thinks, "Ah, here's an easy mark," and he follows up, yapping away, niggling for a fight. I don't like that. Having a very quick temper and being a little bloke, it's a good thing I learned to use my fists in the boxing ring as a kid. I don't come out on top every time, that's for sure, but I win enough to make my point.

Cindy's leg was still floppy, but there was a rubbery sort of connection in the broken bone. I splinted it up again, altering the position of the splint where it had been rubbing her paw. After that I took the bandages off each week and washed them, always keeping Cindy quiet, making her keep still while the splint was off.

The next time I went hunting I took Bouncer with me on a leash. There was a big, very old, bull close to the camp. He seemed to hang around that area and didn't take much notice of me. As cattle tend to stick to their own bit of country I decided to leave him alone for the time being. If later I found I was having trouble getting meat he'd be there, kept in reserve.

We only had to go a couple of miles before I got onto cattle, and shot a cow. She was hit in the shoulder, mortally wounded but taking some time to fall over, so I put Bouncer onto her. He raced in and grabbed her and hung on until she went down, so he got a lot of praise and was very pleased with himself. As far as he was concerned he'd done it all by himself. I don't know what he would have weighed at the time, but he was still quite small, not exactly a bundle of brindle fluff, being short haired, but still more of a pup than anything.

From that cow I took both the rib cages. If you haven't got an ax, you can still get the ribs off in one piece by slicing deep along the line of the backbone with a sharp knife, then taking a firm grip, bracing yourself, and putting everything into a sharp tug against the natural curve of the ribs. They'll snap off. Out of a rib cage I made a sort of basket by cutting holes in the four corners and tying strips of greenhide to it. Into that I piled any loose bits of meat, like fillets, the long straps from the back, and some kidney, making it easier to carry slung over one shoulder. With a forequarter as well it made a pretty heavy load and, as it wasn't too far to go back, I returned for a hindquarter and the second set of ribs.

All the long strips and part of the hindquarter I cut up for more dried meat, not wanting to ever let that run short. Then over the next couple of days ate as much as I could of the fresh meat before it went off, except the rib bones. Hung up in the tree with plenty of air round them, they sealed and kept sweet for longer than any other cuts. You can usually eat rib bones on the fifth or sixth day—providing you don't smell them first, they're very sweet. Once the other meat went off I fed it to the pups for another day or two and then threw the rest out. It depended on the weather and the type of beast how long one kill would last me. Sometimes it was nearly a week. Mostly a lot less. There was always a lot of waste. The crows and kite hawks did well, they soon cleaned up anything that was thrown out, picked the bones bare. They used to hang about the camp, on the lookout, and if I was away for any length of time, would hop into any fresh meat left hanging up. Funnily enough, they didn't bother the strips on the hooks much. When it was really dry, all shrivelled up, they took no notice of it at all. Didn't seem to recognize it for what it was.

It was about this time that I was lying down on the swag one afternoon just looking up at nothing in particular, and I happened to see a tree snake, up in the top branches, just sliding along. He must have been there all the time, but I just hadn't seen him. Once I knew he was there he was easy to see. Sometimes he'd come sliding down a branch across the edge of the platform—one of those real whip-thin, brown fellows, very fast. I don't know what he lived on, although there were a lot of those little mourning doves camped up in the tree, used to fly in every night; they didn't seem to be worried by him. Maybe he ate different gear, I don't really know. But he didn't take much notice of me after he got used to me, and I left him alone. They're very shy as a rule, very hard to catch.

Part Three

Learning How
to Live

Lost

Well, I guess you're the only reason good enough
For what I'm goin' through,
'Cause the only way I walk these miles
Is they might lead back to you.

My head is full of fantasies,
My feet are full of pain
And I've got to hate the sunrise
When I'll stand and walk again.

Well, I can't guess how far I've come
Or how far I've got to go;
But the only exit out of here
Is walkin', that I know.

When first I got stranded here
I thought it was a joke,
But no one saw my blanket flag,
And no one saw my smoke.

I carved the days into a tree,
They slowly circled round;
And if I'd cut another one
It would've fallen down.

Well, Darwin must lie east of here
If I am keepin' true,
I only wish I could find a road
To lead me back to you.

Dyin' would be easy now,
I've got one bullet left;
But I know I'll just keep walkin'
And hopin' for the best.

1

I Explore the River

About a quarter of a mile from the camp the river went
round a sharp bend, the point of the peninsula. At that point
there was a bar going partway across, mainly loose river stones
showing above water at low tide. But there was too much deep
water in channels to make it an effective crossing to the other
side, where the bank sloped up steeply, covered in grass, scrub,
and trees, and then ran on up to the foot of the big ridge.

On my side the peninsula was very dense with trees and
tangled growth pretty well to the water's edge, until, round
the other side, there was an open stretch with a silty beach at
low tide and fairly short grass for about a hundred yards. And
that's where I almost walked onto the biggest crocodile I've ever
seen, because I didn't recognize him.

When you're confronted with something that big it's hard to
recognize it even as being a crocodile. I was just walking along
the edge of the river, casually, just looking around, and the
next thing there was a commotion and this gigantic thing flew
out of the bushes less than a hundred yards ahead, out of the
low growth at the river's edge, and went into the water with

a terrific splash. He must have been in full view for some time and I just didn't realize it could be a crocodile. I suppose he was lying very still. It's hard to estimate the length of a crocodile unless you can step it out, like with the one I'd shot the first day. That was five paces, big paces, making it about sixteen feet, and this one was much, much bigger. Well over twenty feet, and about four across and standing three foot high. Would weigh very close to a ton, I should think. A real monster. Over a hundred years old, at least.

I saw him a few times after that, in the same area, or up in the gorge, when I went there later. An incredibly big lizard. I don't know if he was a danger to me, although I was even more careful with the dogs, but I was quite sure that to have got that big he was very wary himself. He had to be a shy, very cautious sort of a reptile, that would only take game he knew was no danger to himself. He certainly took to the water very fast whenever I got close to him. Perhaps he'd had experience of shooters in the days when crocodile skins were worth a lot of money. Crocodile shooters might have been up the Fitzmaurice then—or on the Victoria, he may have run foul of them there. I think it quite possible for him to have moved from one river system to another. Crocodiles seem to end up in extraordinary places. Sometimes a long way inland you'll find saltwater crocodiles in freshwater billabongs, miles from rivers, so there's no doubt they do a lot of traveling overland during the Wet. Moving from one territory to another.

One time, on the Wongi plains, toward the end of the Wet, we were driving along, more or less overland, off the track, over country which was fairly dry although all the gullies and creeks were full. And we came on a saltie, not a very big one, only about six foot, who was obviously on a cross-country jaunt. He was on a gentle rise, right out in the middle of the open plain, about eight miles out, and doing the old wander.

I know that freshwater crocodiles, the little Johnstone River crocodile which wouldn't hurt a flea, only go short distances into salt water. You'll only see them a little bit down into the tidal influence, whereas the salties seem to live in fresh water for long periods. Sometimes, with old crocs in particular, they get all sorts of marine growths, barnacles and such, on their skins, and they will go upriver to fresh water which kills the marine growth. The barnacles all drop off, and they have a sort of recuperating period before going back into salt water. This was one reason why my area was such a bad one for crocodiles—it was where they seemed to congregate at the meeting of fresh and salt water. The big fellow seemed to stay mainly in the fresh water, and I reckoned he'd been there a long time. And in the case of salties in isolated billabongs, well, they're there for years and years. You would never, hell no, ever take it for granted that just because a billabong is a long way from a river that it won't have a saltwater crocodile in it. In fact some of the biggest specimens seem to end up in secluded billabongs.

A crocodile is a strange animal. For one thing, it doesn't seem to have a distinctive smell to other animals. For example, a dog will bristle up and get excited if you throw a dead snake at it, or will sniff a snake out and either attack it or run about barking as it will at anything strange. But if there's a dead crocodile a dog will come along and walk over it as if it wasn't there. Cattle seem to treat them the same way, take no notice of a croc sunning himself on a bank near where they're feeding. As a crocodile only eats a big meal about once a month, he just lies there and fools the cattle until he wants a feed, then he'll wait at the water's edge and get one.

I was always careful to check the edge of the water to make sure nothing was lying on the bottom. Crocodiles will dig themselves down into the mud, get a good film of mud over their skin and lie on the bottom. Half-buried like that, they're very hard to detect. One way the Aborigines know if a croc's on the bottom is by looking out for "chicken wire." While he's submerged the croc has a big lungful of air that lasts a long time, but he does slowly exhale and his nostrils form two patterns in the shape of chicken wire in the mud. That is the clincher. If you think you've got a crocodile just underwater, and you come to the end of the "log" and there's two chicken wire patches—it's definitely a crocodile. Then you move fast—and the only direction is up.

When a crocodile takes big game, like a cow, it'll grab it by the nose and pull it under, pull it this way and that, and drown it. They have overlocking teeth, two very long ones on the lower jaw which fit into grooves in the upper jaw, made for hanging on or tearing. They can't bite and chew in the normal fashion; small things, fish, birds, small wallabies, they can get down in a couple of bites; but bigger stuff has to get rotten before they can really get into it. Once a dead beast is soft then they can tear pieces off. And they love rotten meat, prefer it to fresh.

Another funny thing, they swallow stones. One theory is that it is a kind of ballast, that the extra weight lets them lie on the bottom more easily. And never be fooled by them looking so slow and sleepy, they move like lightning when they want, and can use their tail as a whip to lash something into the water. They can even get up a fair sort of a gallop across land for short distances, outrun most people, no trouble at all.

Once the oar was finished—maybe paddle is a better word for it—I was able to use the dinghy again. The homemade job wasn't very flash, but it was light and strong enough for what I needed. With the next incoming tide I went to see what the river was like further upstream, having been only a couple of miles in that direction along the bank. Going by water was a lot less effort, and quicker. I could go up on one tide, and come back when it did.

For about six miles along its course the river continued to take enormous bends, almost doubling back on itself, with the first one just up from the camp. Shortly after that the ridge was gone, and with other hills a fair way off, that far side was a low flood plain, covered with tall cane grass, six foot high. There was another kind of grass or reed growing into the waterline along some sections. Very dark and dense, with a fronded head, it looked a bit like pictures of that reed the old-time Egyptians used to make paper out of—papyrus. The fronded heads bent over, shadowing the water, and there were little tunnels here and there where wallabies and wild pig had made their way through to drink. Very dark and mysterious-looking. And there were much larger tunnels, ending in a slippery dip on the smooth muddy bank. Crocodile slides. Where they like to lie and sun themselves, with a quick takeoff into the water down the slide.

There were one or two sand islands along the way. Very clean and shining in the sun. A couple of crocs asleep on one. Mother and child, by the look of them. They didn't take much notice of me, nor of the blue crane and other water birds pottering about in the shallows. Just as well for the birds, crocodiles being quite fond of feathered gear for the odd snack.

On my side, the south, the banks were mostly cut very high and sheer, plunging straight down, and a brilliant shade of red. So bright that it reflected in the water. In places there was weathering, probably started when flooding had scoured into the bank, which had then worn into collections of weird peaks and pinnacles. It was all very interesting, but I couldn't see much beyond the banks because of being right down on water level, except that the hills were closing in on the river again, especially on the far side where another big ridge came down.

Not far past that the river ran into a gorge, which had another partial bar just before it, breaking the flow to some degree and causing it to widen a little. The far banks were high again, running back into hills with a lot of trees and growth on them, while on the south, where the hills came in at an angle, it was flat just at that point. Very heavy with tangled grass, cane, paperbark trees, pandanus palms, and peppermint trees. And in the middle, a perfect landing place. A clearing in all the growth, well eaten down and with cattle pads wandering down to the water. A good place to stop, but I went further up the gorge first.

The first section was a pretty stretch of river, lined with trees, vines and grasses, all very lush, with rocky hills just behind. Then the rock closed in and the gorge was very deep, very dark green water, running past high cliffs and colorful rock formations, red-brown and yellowish. The pockets of vegetation were real rain forest, the big trees smothered in vines, some of them cascading like a green wall right into the water. A very picturesque place, and the river must be a helluva depth all along there. That could be one reason why, even with an incoming tide, the water stays fairly fresh for some way downstream. There is just such a volume of fresh water coming down against it.

The tide pretty well stopped inside the gorge, so, after a bit of rowing, I drifted back to pull in at the clearing I'd seen earlier. Pulled the dinghy up, and went off to have a look about. The clearing was about a hundred yards long and not quite as wide, all short-cropped grass, completely enclosed by cane grass and trees.

I followed a cattle pad through the cane grass and came onto a stand of huge wild fig trees, with an open flood plain beyond, going back toward the nearest bend in the river. The fig trees were really noble specimens, with buttressed gray trunks and great branches meeting right overhead. An ideal campsite, and it was well used by cattle. That was good, I'd know where to get meat if hunting got too hard near my camp.

The cane grass was full of wallabies, whole families of them lurking in its thick shelter, which was a maze of their pathways and camping spots. They were all the agile wallaby, a pretty animal, light fawn-colored, with distinct dark markings on the face, like a mask. Some of them grow quite big for a wallaby, big as a small kangaroo, and they are exceptionally nippy on their feet, hence their name, agile. They are found all over the North, very thick in some parts. Carlton Hill, a station out of Kununurra, gets the biggest mobs of them coming into the compound round the homestead buildings. So many the whole ground looks like it's on the move. Up to fifty get onto the lawn the manager is trying to grow round his house, all at once, all hoeing into the one poor little patch of green. And yet you'll rarely see a dead wallaby by the side of the road. Unlike the kangaroo, which tends to jump into a car's headlights at night, the wallaby always manages to skip out of the way at the last moment, even when a car is traveling fast. They have very short forearms which they carry stuck straight out in front of them, not tucked in, and keep their very long tail well up and straight out when doing any speed.

The agile wallaby is the commonest marsupial in the Fitzmaurice area, but I did see a few nail-tail wallabies while I was there, very curious little animals with a sort of bony spur on the tip of their tail. I'm not too sure what it's there for, although it might be used for grooming purposes. There were also some kangaroos, not many, and the solid, stocky walleroos or euros in the hills. That just about wrapped up the marsupial line of things.

But the area near the gorge isn't just popular with wallabies and cattle. It's a fantastic spot for birds, with the big fig trees, thick growth, and tall cane grass, the proximity of open plain, river and hills, it's got something for all kinds and has a terrific concentration of bird life. I saw all kinds of finches, gouldians, plum-heads, double-bars, and zebras, a few star finches, and a lot of blood finches. A few brolgas were there, not many, and I only saw two emus during the whole time.

I saw a big mob of blue-winged kookaburras, very much like the normal kookaburra in size and shape, but with a lot of blue in the back and wings. They sound like a kookaburra gone wrong, or just practicing for the first time, a crazy, shrieking cackle. There were a few little kingfishers, with bright blue backs and white underparts, a lot of brown pigeons, doves, and the usual collection of cockatoos and parrots. Wrens, flycatchers, blood finches, all sorts of little birds in the cane grass, and, swooping over the plain, bee-eaters or rainbow-birds: very pretty little birds, green, pale blue and golden bronze, with a distinctive call, a sort of descending purring whistle. There were butcher-birds, honey-eaters, warblers, the mud-lark who seems to be found everywhere, and even a couple of white and gray sea-eagles nesting over above the gorge. A big-time bird-watcher would have his work cut out for weeks. Up in the fig trees there were bower-birds, looking for ripe figs, of which there weren't many, just the odd one changing from hard green to soft dusty pink. Not very appetizing gear even when ripe, in my opinion, but I reckoned once the sun went down, those trees would be full of flying foxes (the fruit-bats who camped on the far side of the river during the day).

I was very pleased with everything I saw just around there, except for one thing. The plain was covered by a dark green, broad leaved, bushy sort of a plant. Bloody rubber bush—calotropis, an introduced plant which has escaped custody. Got out and into the bush, all over the place, and in the usual fashion with anything we don't much want, it's doing very well

for itself. Everywhere, a dead-set pest. It's not exactly poison-
ous to stock, but it's not any good as feed either. Not even any
good as firewood. The stuff can grow as big as a small tree,
but a branch is like a chunk of dried-out sponge. Burns all right,
but you'd need a truckload to boil a billy. It was a bit of a
shock to see that the blasted thing had spread as far as the
Fitzmaurice, right out there in wild country, and had got such
a hold, too. Feral plants are just as much of a menace in their
own way as feral animals.

The far side of the plain, inland from the river, was flanked
by a sandy ridge covered with medium-sized timber—kadji-
but, coolibah, stringybark, and spotted gum—and there were
cattle moving through it and down onto the plain. I moved back
toward the river before they saw me; no point in disturbing
them at that time, when I had meat in the camp.

The next day I rowed over to the other side of the river,
tied the boat up, and then set out to climb the big ridge. It
was steep, but a slight gully running up at one point made it
reasonably easy climbing. Just the last section was a matter of
scrambling up over rocks to get to the flat top. There was certainly a fantastic view. I could see the river winding back like
a giant green snake until it disappeared into the coastal haze.
Upstream I could see the gorge, and then the river going
through some dense sort of rain forest with more rough country beyond. To the north it was just plain rough, hills and ridges
and big jump-ups in lines of violet blue, getting paler and paler
to nothing. And to the south, beyond the flood plains and low
rises, the open flats and timbered grass lands, the bad country
began again. My area was, in fact, a pocket of good country,
a kind of oasis in the wilderness, extending about ten miles to
the south and hemmed in on all sides by very rough stuff
indeed.

It was a clear, bright day. I could see more than twenty miles in all directions, and in every direction there was nothing but wild country. A bit depressing, it was, sitting up there just taking it all in. Any faint possibility that might have crossed my mind about some musterers turning up, from anywhere, from Bradshaw if it was their country, was dispelled by that view. The cattle in the area had made their way in through the ranges, and it was highly unlikely that anyone would try to get them out again. I'd really known that all along, because of the wild state of the cattle. Not a single brand or earmark, no cut bullocks. One old bull had once had his horns tipped—that was the only sign of anyone having ever tried to handle them.

The buildup of bulls in the herd, and the number of black-faced ones among them, was another sure indication. Somewhere, away back, the old shorthorn stock must have some black blood in them, and it comes out when they go wild for a long period, especially noticeable in the solid reds. The basic red color runs into black over the neck and head, and they also get very leggy and light in the hindquarters, with powerful forequarters. Start to look like the classic fighting bulls. And very cranky, bad-tempered bastards they are, too. A wild bull won't usually go for you unless provoked, although it would be most unwise to trust any of them. The black-faced bulls are the most untrustworthy of the lot.

When cattle have been running wild for too long they also tend to an imbalance of the sexes. There are too many bulls in proportion to the cows, and when a cow comes on heat she can be maimed or killed by the number of bulls getting onto her. The result is that the more fertile cows don't always live to reproduce, leaving a higher percentage of barren cows or those which don't come into season every year. The cow population drops back while the bulls increase, until eventually the herd goes into a decline. Nature's way of dealing with overpopulation, probably. There were some beautiful cattle on the Fitzmaurice, but once the numbers reached a certain peak they would then start to go downhill.

I found out later that they handle their cattle well on Bradshaw, but that, sure enough, the problems involved with trying to get cattle out of the Fitzmaurice had meant that they had tried to muster there only twice in the last twelve years. And without much success.

Halfway down the ridge I met Bouncer, dripping wet. He'd chewed through his rawhide leash and come after me. Swum the river. He didn't know how lucky he was to have made it across. A couple of mornings before I'd heard a hell of a splash and a flurry in the water, had grabbed the rifle and raced to the bank, where the pup had been playing. Thought: "Hell, a croc's got him." It was a wallaby. It must have been feeding along the lower bank, just feeding along, not noticing anything until it was face to face with Bouncer. So it had taken fright and jumped, out into the river. And was then swimming like mad for the other side. Swimming like a puppy dog, flat out. I didn't know they could swim like that, but it was doing fine, making very good time. Until it got halfway across—then pfft! it vanished. Not even a ripple. Something pulled it under, straight down.

So Bouncer was lucky he'd made it. And so was I. Couldn't afford to lose him.

2

Remembering Things Past

I started making a spear. I'd need one eventually, I thought, so had better see how it turned out. A tree root was the only thing long enough, straight and strong enough. There are exposed roots along the riverbank, where the soil has been washed away, and I dug out about eight foot of one and chopped it off. Then heated it over the fire to dry it out, slowly, taking a couple of days. As it bent one way I'd turn it the other, until in the end it was very straight and hard, but still springy. That's the only sort of spear which would bring down a beast. You can make them out of strong cane, but they're only good for small game, like a wallaby, or fish. I did kill a wallaby with a cane spear, but if I ever needed to spear cattle, I had to have something heavier.

I was pretty confident that when the time came I would be able to bring a cow down with what I had made. I could find a cattle pad passing under a tree, climb up and wait for a cow to pass under, then drop down and drive the spear in. Or maybe make a trap, using the rope. As a last resort, if I wounded a beast in the hindquarters I could then follow it up, pull it down by the tail, and cut its throat. The spear was there in case I ran out of ammunition or if the dogs couldn't hunt for some reason.

There were times when I felt depressed about the whole situation, but then that would go when something seemed to work out as I had hoped. I wasn't at any stage exactly looking forward to the whole thing, but it was, not exciting, but challenging, to be able to live under those conditions. And when something did work out it was a step further in the knowledge that I could survive there, and I enjoyed that.

I suppose I'd consider myself an average bushman, but average by old-time standards. I can think of plenty of old-time bushmen who would survive where I was and not think very much of it at all. Some younger ones with the same standards, too. They'd be all right. But even in the bush, things are changing and a lot of the old ways and attitudes have gone to a fair extent. Some of the young blokes coming into the bush just don't get the chance to learn what they should.

That sounds like someone from another generation talking, but, as the bush is old-fashioned to the city, so I guess my attitude is even old-fashioned to a lot of people in the bush today. Which is probably due to two things, mainly my upbringing . . . especially the early years on Jo Jo, where the influence of the Old Man and Uncle Les was very strong. And it went back almost two generations, because the old men in Southern Queensland who had taught Les about the bush were very old-fashioned. Lived in slab houses, made out of slab timber, made their own greenhide whips and gear, stuck to the old ways. They were three brothers, the Hunts, and they had a very slow, drawling, old-fashioned way of talking: "Goodness, gracious me, boy." Never said there was a lot of, or even mobs of, anything. It was always "a power of timber," "a power of cattle," and they never called a wallaby a wallaby. It was always "a power of marsupials on the flat."

Well, Uncle Les left that influence to go more or less straight into a situation where he was very isolated from then on, so he kept up the old ways, which were the best for handling cattle in the kind of country Jo Jo was then. Growing up with the influence of my father and Uncle Les, and handed down through them, the Hunts, I gained their attitudes to the bush.

I always looked up to my father and Les. They were both very good at what they did, with horses, cattle, and other bush work, and I never knew either of them to chicken out of anything they set out to do.

My father taught me to ride when I was about four or five, and my brothers and sisters. That was doing cattle work, pushing up the tail of the mob, that kind of thing, on quiet horses. But my four cousins learned to ride much earlier than that. Aunty Nell, Les's wife, who is a marvelous horsewoman, used to carry the babies in a sling around her neck when she was riding, so they absolutely grew up on horses, and can all ride very well indeed.

Uncle Les hardly ever goes into town—it's a pretty ratshit dirt road, and a long way—he doesn't drink or smoke so he doesn't go in to pubs. And he won't read newspapers—all lies, he says. And until recent years there was no homestead on Jo Jo. He lived in a covered wagon, one of those chuck wagons with a canvas top. Then the Company insisted on a homestead being built. So it was, a big flash homestead, and Les flatly refused to live in it.

In their heyday, when they were really getting a lot of scrubbers off Jo Jo, they had at least sixty bullterriers on the place. This was because, throwing bulls, they'd take a team of ten or twelve dogs with them every day. Now ten or twelve dogs, you use them once a fortnight, and that's it. Out of that number, two might get killed, two get broken legs, and the rest are so battered and bruised they probably won't get home that day, but straggle back in twos and threes over several days.

Sometimes the dogs would be used to help throw the bulls, if it was real thick country where it was hard to get at a bull. Sometimes they'd gallop along with the horsemen, when it was early in the day, but later, when they got a bit tired, they would stick with the mob, which was where they were the biggest asset. Their main purpose was to keep the bulls which had been thrown and de-horned in with the coachers. As soon as a bull was let into the mob the dogs would be waiting for him to break out, knowing what was up. And as soon as a bull broke out the dogs would be onto him. Go straight in and hit him and hang on, seven or eight dogs like a mob of ticks, until the bull went down, and still hang on. The bull would then get up and dash back into the mob and once he did that the dogs would drop off. After doing that a couple of times the bulls could decide it's safer to stay with the mob rather than break out and bail up and cause all sorts of trouble.

They were throwing bulls every day at that stage, hence the vast number of dogs, just to be able to keep throwing bulls. They had hollow logs cut for kennels, rows and rows of hollow logs, and dogs tied up to every one. Even now I'd guarantee they'd have twenty or thirty dogs on the place, even when they're not doing much scrub-running.

A dog wasn't allowed to bark. It could chew a visitor's leg right off but it couldn't bark. With sixty dogs, if you let one bark it'd be bedlam. They'd all bark. Uncle Les had a small-gauge shotgun, and if a dog barked it got a charge from it. It didn't matter whose dog it was, or whether it was a good, bad, or indifferent dog—if it barked, it got a charge. Which didn't kill it but was certainly a very painful experience and the dog generally remembered.

Unfortunately the toilet, which was just the usual tin-shed affair, was situated in the midst of those dog kennels. So if you wanted to go to the toilet in the middle of the night, you snuck very carefully up through the dog kennels—"Shhhh dog, shhhhh dog"—and if a dog barked you headed for the toilet at a flat gallop because sure enough the barrel of the shotgun would poke out of the canvas wagon and "Kerboom!" in the general direction. You'd move fairly fast.

Both my sisters went on to finish their formal education. Jennifer is a teacher and Christine a secretary. But both my brother and I left school at fifteen and sixteen respectively, and Malcom is now a cattle buyer. I couldn't see the sense in school, which isn't to say I was right, but that's how I felt, although it's a good thing that I was made to go, I suppose. But, with the kind of life and work I have, what I learned from being on Jo Jo and from my father, working with him at Murgon, is more valuable than what I learned at school. And there is another reason why I have the kind of attitude I do—my determination to lead a fairly solitary existence.

I like people, meeting them, talking to them, but when I'm working in the bush I like to live with it; to do that you've got to make as little intrusion upon it as possible. It's best to be by yourself . . . maybe it's got something to do with being in tune with the land, something like that. And I've found that if you're going to meet the bush on fairly solitary terms without a great deal of capital behind you, then the old ways are still the best ways. All that kind of thing was standing me in good stead on the Fitzmaurice.

Although the thought did cross my mind that if I hadn't been like that I would never have ended up in such a situation in the first place.

3

Night Solitude

The nights were rarely silent. There's a stillness, but that's not the same thing, and every sound carries for miles. I had to get up through the night to put more wood on the fire, keeping it burning, sometimes sit by it for a bit, listening to the sounds of the bush. A mopoke up in the timber somewhere, the boobook owl, a monotonous gentle call. Curlews down by the river, a very high-pitched and somehow thin-sounding cry, with a drawn out upward flick at the end: "Ker-leee ker-leee."

The bulls usually had a few words to say. I could hear them grumbling on their way to water further downstream, then stopping to have an argument. A couple of old bulls could go on for hours, snorting and coughing and wheezing insults at one another, then working up from a low deep angry mumbling to break out into terrific shrieks and brassy bellows. If they were on the right spot the echoes from the ridge would bounce back across the river, and probably wake up some of the blue-winged kookaburras who'd join in with a few cackles and yells of their own. If there was any sort of a moon the noise would go on all night—it seemed to stir them all up.

There were dingoes, too. Plenty of dingoes about, but the ones on the far side of the river were a pretty lean and hungry lot, there being no cattle over there. They used to smell the meat from my camp and come down to the river's edge and howl, but never tried to get across, no doubt having too much respect for the crocodiles.

Usually a pack of dingoes will howl all together only once or twice during the night, and that is one of the most beautiful sounds in the bush. High and wild and sad, really beautiful. Then they will often be heard howling again at sunrise, calling to one another as the pack joins up again.

I'd almost always get up at daylight. Get up and put a big mob of wood on the fire, and then go down to the river for a wash and a drink. Quite often there'd be a couple of dogs sitting straight across the river. They'd have been poking up or down the river and smelled the camp, smelled me, the meat, and the other dogs, and sat there, curious, on the other side, until daylight. They were aware of me all right, but definitely weren't afraid, just curious. I'd walk out along the riverbank and they'd look at me, sort of stand up and trot one way, then look at me again; they didn't gallop off in mad fright. Got a lot of curiosity, dingoes. They were all yellow dogs, but went from a deep ginger right through to a sort of washed-out whitish color.

One morning I heard cattle bellow out just before daylight. As soon as I could see I went out, reckoned I could find them. And came across a couple of weaner buffalo feeding right on the edge of the river, just where the banks are pretty high. I thought, right, I'll roll one of these buggers over, and I got one, right in the butt of the ear, and he sort of lurched forward, then over he went, rolled down the bank and into the river. That was no good, there was no way I was going to stagger in after a bleeding buffalo and start carving him up in that water. So I left him there, which was a pity, but definitely wiser.

I forgot about him, but about a week later I could hear dingoes howling, right back in the distance, and they seemed to come up the river, real slow, howling, howling, but getting closer all the time. So I thought, "What's up with this mob?" and poked over to the bank and had a look across. And there's this buffalo, he's bloated up fat as a drum and floating up the river, and the dingoes are trotting along the bank, following him, waiting for him to be pushed into the bank so they could get him. Went trotting right past the camp following that buffalo, and a scrawny hungry-looking lot they were, too. They couldn't have got him, because the next day he floated back down with the outgoing tide, and that blasted buffalo floated back and forth for days. There's a half hour difference in tides, so it'd be a bit later each day, and the last time I saw him was midday, and that time he floated past with a couple of crocodiles floating with him, feeding off the rotten meat underneath.

I saw a mob of dingoes hunting, another morning. Hunting pig. I heard the pigs squealing over the other side of the river, and there was one pig with a big white spot on the shoulder, and two dogs took off after that, flat out. I could see the heavy grass rustling and waving as the pig went through, and the dogs sort of bounding through it, so they were going rather slowly. They went out of sight, up round the bend in the river, and I thought no more about it, until about three quarters of an hour later, more commotion on the other side, and the same pig comes past with the white spot on the shoulder, and there's a different dog after it this time—just one big solid yellow dog.

Well, he took it for another three quarters of an hour. They must have been running it in a circle, out round the bend of the river, round the ridge and back again. And up on the top of the hill were four or five dogs, and while the pig and the dogs that were chasing it were going round the base of the ridge at ninety, these other ones were just trotting round the top with only a fraction of the distance to cover, going round. And when one dog got puffed out, apparently a fresh one would fly down the ridge and pick up the chase, give the pig a bit more of a gallop. And they got him, no worries. Killed him.

I often wondered how they'd catch an animal like that; must use the same method with wallabies, because a wallaby's got a lot more pace than a dog, so that's the only way they'd get them, just run them in relays, get them to go in a circle and have one dog following their tail, with the other one taking shortcuts all the time.

They certainly work in packs or pairs when attacking cattle, especially in getting a cow away from her calf. One dog will tease the cow, snap at her until she chases after it, and a dog or dogs will stay behind to kill the calf. Then they'll wait until the cow leaves the dead calf before eating it. In some areas they cause heavy losses among cattle, and will quite successfully attack and pull down beasts up to weaner size. You'll see quite a few cattle, grown beasts, with stumpy tails. They are the ones that got away.

They're a savage animal, dingoes, and one of the few that will kill for the pleasure of it. They do enormous damage in sheep country, and will go into a mob of sheep and kill or maim dozens and eat the livers out of just a few. And they often kill rather messily, if they catch a weaner or something like that, a lot of times they don't kill it, virtually eat it alive. Pull the animal down, hamstring it, and then more or less just start in eating it, don't bother about killing it. Very cruel hunters, dingoes.

I know some people have a theory that dingoes don't kill larger animals much at all, that they live on rats and grasshoppers. I think that's an area thing, depending on what country it is, and what game is there, and what stock. Wallabies, for example, are a helluva lot faster than a beast, and a lot harder to catch, so if there's cattle or sheep about, the dingo finds it easier to eat them, just as he'd find it easier than trying to feed on rats and grasshoppers. There'd have to be a lot of rats and grasshoppers about before he'd prefer catching them to cattle and sheep. Maybe some of the needless slaughter is the training of young dogs to hunt, but there's no doubt a lot of it is for the pleasure of killing.

Yet I wouldn't like to see the dingo wiped out. A healthy dingo is a handsome animal, and the sound of a pack howling out in wild country on a clear moonlit night is one of the most beautiful things you can hear in the bush.

4

Dawn and the Daily Round

Dawn would be just a faint glow in the darkness beyond the river, with the stars still shining and then starting to fade as the light moved up until it caught the tops of trees and turned the river into one sheet of sparkling silver. From the first hint of light the birds would be on the move, calling, crying, singing, flying out to their feeding grounds. A very active time of day for all living things. That would be the time I'd hear the call of the bush pheasant, down by the river in thick cover, a sort of deep drumming sound. They usually only call at dawn and sunset. A fairly heavy reddish brown bird, with a long tail, that stays low to the ground even if it takes off to fly.

Soon after getting up and putting wood on the fire, if I was going to hunt, I'd check the wind out. See which way it was blowing, and from that decide which direction I would take. All sorts of complexities arise when you're hunting. A strong cold wind means there's a lot of places not worth looking for cattle. I'd decide, perhaps, if it was a real cold windy morning, and there were a few of those, that there'd be some sheltered spots not too far from the camp where cattle would hide. Depressions like dried billabongs that'd be out of the wind.

I'd touch up the knives before I went, stone and steel them until I could shave with them, shave the hairs off my arm anyway. That'd take some time. Then I'd get out of my jeans and jacket. I used to wear them at night for the warmth, but strip down to shorts for hunting. Not too good, on a cold morning, getting out of a nice warm jacket, but it was just too noisy wearing it. Then away I'd go, often taking some of the dried meat with me to chew on while I was out. Once I got onto cattle I'd walk right round to the back of them, swing right round to keep on the right side of the wind. If I was lucky I'd get a beast early. Would then make a couple trips to get everything back into the camp, maybe four or five miles, get meat hung up and strips hung for drying, and by then it'd be late, the hottest part of the day. So I'd have a bit of a camp. Then when it was cooler go and look for berries, get more firewood, and cut more fresh branches to keep a stack of green stuff handy in case I needed to make a smoke signal. The only sign of a plane I had had was the sound of a jet away in the distance a couple of times, but if a light plane came along I had to have the green branches ready, at all times, to throw on the fire. Then there was the rope, which had to be twisted up regularly as it slackened off, to keep it taut.

Sometimes I was flat out getting everything done that I wanted to do before sundown. And it gets dark pretty early and very quick up in the North at that time of the year. One minute the sun is going down all gold and red and all the country, the trees and hills and river, are washed over in a burnished light, and then it's gone. Just a reflected glow in the west, and a gathering haze of soft colors, the birds all making a last-minute racket, and then it's dark. The crickets take over, chirping away like mad, there's the first curlew crying, a bull starting to rumble and bellow somewhere in the distance, and the stars are coming out in a deep blue sky. In no time at all there are thousands of stars, stretched across from one horizon to another.

There were other days when I didn't have much to do at all, just take a wander through the bush, or sit and think. And nothing to do at night but sit by the fire . . . and think. Something I hadn't counted on, hadn't given a thought to, was that I got lonely. Which isn't the same as being depressed. To me they're two quite different emotions. I got depressed if I went out hunting and didn't get a beast, if things didn't work out right, but there was always the next day, and that would be better. But I found I got lonely when everything else was all right, beef in the camp, nothing to worry about. With nothing else to occupy my mind, I would start thinking about people, and get lonely. So I talked to the dogs, I reckoned it was all right so long as they didn't talk back at me. If they did that I'd be in trouble. If I hadn't had the dogs I would have had to have got a pet of some kind, a young bird, or wallaby, a calf; something to talk to, to give some sort of affection.

I wrote a lot of poetry—well, made it up and committed it to memory, not having anything to write on. When it comes to that, I never have written much of it down, although I've always liked composing it. One thing about not putting verses on paper, you can change lines any time you like. I made up more than ever before while on the Fitzmaurice, although not a lot of it was actually about that situation, but it was a way of keeping aware of what was going on, in the bush, and in general. Quite a bit of it was romantic, because I'm a romantic at heart, I suppose. Not necessarily directed at anyone in particular, not all of the time. Just romantic. Missing company was one thing, missing women on a male-female basis was another. I don't think I'd ever go in for a celibate way of life, not voluntarily.

Some of the poems were a way of looking back, remembering things about how man started off as a hunter, has lived and hunted off the land from time immemorial, with really early man the basic hunter. Until he changed over, became useless at looking after himself away from the protection of his society. Once he built villages and started growing crops, had a base he had to return to, then that was the start of civilization. And now he's been slowly alienated from what he started off as. Maybe that's part of the frustration people find now—because the male animal is the basic hunter, the survivor, and men still have those instincts from their early beginnings.

Making up poems made me think things out, it was a mental discipline, having to pin things down. Some of them were more lyrics for songs rather than poems, but it was all along the general lines of verse rather than prose, because that's the way I like to express things. Poetry, bush poetry, and bush songs, have always been a part of my background. Up at Jo Jo, Uncle Les used to recite bush poetry and sing, and play the mouth organ, and there was a half-caste bloke, Leo Pope, who played the guitar, and we all used to sing to that. It was, if you like, all very much the old traditional bush culture. From Banjo Patterson and Henry Lawson to songs and verse just handed down or made up on the spot. I hated school, but from a pretty early age I could recite most of Patterson and Lawson from memory.

There weren't many books out at Jo Jo, but at Murgon there were always books, and all of the family, except me, learned to play at least one musical instrument well. Not me, music just isn't my line of country. But my father and I used to yarn for hours, swapping stories, old bush stories, that had been sort of handed down for years. Or he'd tell me about things that had happened before I could remember. A bush yarn can be about anything—people, places, things that happened, anything—sad, funny, wild, or just plain ridiculous. And that has always been a very old-time, traditional bush entertainment.

I remember one time, when I was very small, they all set up a trap for cattle in a place called Windy Valley. Had a yard set up and a swinging gate with a great length of plain wire going up through the limbs of trees to the top of the ridge. When there were enough cattle in it they were going to pull the wire and close the gate. I was very small, but I remember it was a very moonlit night and about three in the morning. We were all shivering there, and the time's right. Enough cattle in the yard.

So they pulled the wire, and it got caught. Stuck in too many forks and bends down to the gate. So they decided to sneak down and close the gate by hand. I was told to stay where I was, which I did, but Uncle Les and the Old Man and two other blokes, Teddy and Hobbsy, snuck down this valley. Just got to the gate when the wind changed and a hundred head of scrub cattle smelled them and, of course, spun straight round and galloped out. Well, Hobbsy dived behind a log and the Old Man and Les went behind a big bark tree and Teddy shot up a sapling. Which, it turned out, wasn't thick enough, and the higher he went the more it bent over, so as those scrub cattle went under they were bumping him on the way. He was clinging like a koala for dear life underneath. Just as the last beast went past, the sapling broke and he fell on the ground. They reckoned you never saw a bloke with a grip on a sapling like it. They had to pry it out of his hands.

There was another time, when we were out riding, and Teddy was on a colt called Osti, who could buck a bit. Well, the dogs got onto a goanna, and chased it, and the goanna ran up the first tall thing it saw, as is their wont, and it happened to be the colt Osti. The goanna ran straight up the back of the horse, and of course clung to his rump with its sharp claws, and there was nothing the horse could do but duck its head and buck. The dogs kept pouring in after the goanna and it was a real shemozzle. Teddy got thrown, the goanna went off with the bucking horse, clinging to the saddle, and the dogs racing alongside, barking. Took hours to get it all sorted out. By the time we captured the horse the goanna had come off somewhere along the line, but he was sticking some pretty good bucks the last time we saw him. Riding a lot better than Teddy, we reckoned.

5

Bees and Other Wildlife

I've got what you might call a sweet tooth, the sweetest ever. If no one's looking I'll put six spoons of sugar in my tea, that kind of thing. And I was missing sugar, bad. Not just because of itself, but also because of stamina. Without sugar I found that, although I still had plenty of strength, and I felt fit enough, I was starting to lose stamina. Got knocked up more quickly than I used to if I had to run a long way after cattle or anything like that.

I knew there was a nest of wild bees about. There aren't a lot of bush bees in that country, but I'd seen a few, but couldn't find the nest. Down South, where they've got the introduced bee, the big fellow, out in the bush, you can often find nests with the biggest mobs of honey. Go round tapping on hollow logs for a while and they'll find you, being pretty vicious turn-outs. But there aren't any introduced bees in the North, and the native bee is a tiny little black fellow, smaller than a housefly, and he doesn't sting. The entrance hole to his nest is a lot smaller than the top of your little finger, just the tiniest opening into a tree trunk or branch. Impossible to find, for a

white man. An Aboriginal has a very good eye, a much better
eye than a whitefellow, and he can follow them. Not the one
bee, because they fly at about forty miles an hour, but he'll
find where they're drinking, watch one take off and follow it.
When he loses sight of that bee he waits at the same spot for
the next one to come past, because the bees will always take
the shortest line between their nest and water. When the next
one comes past, he runs after that, and so on, until he finds
the nest. But my eyesight's not that good.

My camp was in line between the bees' nest and the river,
and after a bit they got lazy. Instead of going all the way to
the river they started to drink at the dog's water tin. Kids in
Queensland will catch the bigger bees at horse troughs, tangle
a bit of cotton wool in their legs, and then find their nest that
way, because any idiot could follow a bee carrying a big blob
of white cotton wool. You can't do quite the same thing with
the native bee, he's too small, but I'd been shown how to stick
a bit of cotton to one with gum, any kind of resinous gum from
a tree, which slows him down so he can just get off the ground
and putter along. That, and a bit of cotton being easier to see
than a pinhead of a bee, make it about the only way a whitefellow will find their nest. The only other way is if a bee comes
and taps him on the shoulder and says, "Over here."

I had strands of cotton from the shirt I'd torn up to bandage
the dog's leg, bees coming in to drink at the tin, and all the
time in the world. I caught about ten bees before I found one
that felt like co-operating enough and I had the cotton the right
length. He took off and crashed to the ground about ten yards
from the camp, and that was the end of him, because when I
galloped up to the spot, I trod on him. Squashed the poor little bugger flat. So, back to the water tin. It took nearly all day,
but in the end everything worked, and I found the nest, only
about forty yards from the camp. Had a feed of honey, got

into it with the knife, cut round the branch it was in and broke it off and gouged the nest out with the knife. Which was a short-term sort of action. If I'd been thinking properly, considered for a minute, I'd have only made a small hole and got a piece of hollow cane grass and shoved it up into the little honey pouch in the nest. Then I could have had a bit every day. But for some reason I forgot that at the time. Honey. Food. Sugar. Attacked it wild. And that was the only nest I found.

By about the end of the fourth week I'd explored most of the area out from my camp on my side of the river—all the good country to where the hills started to come in again. Partly because I had to know it reasonably well when hunting, where cattle were likely to go under certain weather conditions, all that kind of thing, and I had to know what else was there, in the way of game and other food. And anyway, I enjoyed looking around, seeing what could be seen. Have always been interested in the bush, the animals in it and the way they live in their little societies, and their relationship to their environment.

Where I was, I had more time to observe, and I appreciated being able to have that time. It was interesting to see how close I could get to a wallaby without it taking fright, and I could spend as long as I liked stalking one. You can get very close if you take it quietly, don't lift your hands or make any movement that looks suspicious from the wallaby's point of view. Just stand straight and go forward very slowly; if the wallaby thumps the ground with his foot, thump back with your foot. He'll usually decide you're another wallaby and go on feeding again.

At one stage, out of Murgon, I used to catch animals for a zoo which was starting up out of Brisbane. Caught them wallabies, goannas, snakes, birds. For a zoo, they had to be alive and well, beaming with good health. Caught forty scrub-turkeys—not the plain turkey, the Australian bustard, but the scrub-turkey who's like a smaller version of the domestic turn-out. The zoo people said they'd take any amount, so I took them literally and sent down forty. They were a bit aston-ished, but accepted them all, and now I believe the turkeys are breeding; must be the biggest collection of scrub-turkeys any-where in the world, I'd reckon.

I found that the buffaloes, which hadn't been numerous in the first place, seemed to have moved out. Unlike cattle, which tend to keep to a certain area, the buffaloes are wanderers, and have come right across from Arnhem Land and other parts of the Territory, across into Western Australia. The odd one has turned up as far west as Kununurra and they've also poked down as far as Hooker Creek, on the edge of the desert country.

As far as trees and plants went, there are quite a few in that country whose names I don't know, but I did find one unusual thing, a stand of pines—the dark green bush pine—growing along a section of the higher riverbank. They're common fur-ther south, but I don't know of any others anywhere near that area. There were heath-type shrubs of various kinds, vines and creepers on a lot of trees, and a few staghorns, not very big specimens, but doing all right. As well as pandanus there were a couple of other types of palms, or cycads, like zamia palms. It is a pretty mixed kind of vegetation, one of everything and two of most.

One bush to avoid is an ordinary gray looking shrub, caus-tic bush, which brings you out in blisters if you brush against it. And it's best not to knock against a green tree-ants' nest, either—they're a brilliant emerald green little ant, make a sort of bag out of leaves stuck together and get pretty annoyed if disturbed. They have a fiery sting, which doesn't last long but makes you jump at the time.

Speaking of ants, there are a lot of ant-lions in that country.

For their size they're as ferocious as a genuine lion. Their traps were all over the place, little funnel-shaped hollows in soft soil or sand, about as big across as an eggcup. The ant-lion—who's actually the larva stage of the lacewing insect—sits at the bottom, a tiny weeny little creature, and mostly jaws at that. When an ant slips down the side of the slope the ant-lion helps it on its way down by flicking a shower of sand grains over it, then grabs it in its pincers and pulls it under. They seem to tackle any ant from the smallest to the biggest meat-ants x times their own size.

I didn't find many birds' eggs, as most of them nest in prickly bushes or high up in tall trees. And the bower-bird's nest I found wasn't really a nest; a penthouse is more like it. The male builds it, a curved, tidy-looking tunnel affair, on the ground, made out of grass and sticks. Spread out in the entrance were all the goodies he'd collected, small stones and leaves and snail shells. Anything that had caught his eye. Very fussy about his collection too, the bower-bird, gets very upset if you muck up his flash arrangements and will spend hours putting everything back where it belongs. The bower isn't a nest in the true sense, it's a display area for the male, a place to impress his girl friend.

The only feed of eggs I had was when I found a plain turkey's nest. There are quite a few plain turkeys around there, tall fawn and gray birds with black "caps" on their heads, fairly slow moving. I shot one to eat as well, thinking a change from red meat might not be a bad thing. It was good, too, because the turkey had a big full crop, full of grain, cockatoo-grass seed, and stuff like that. I opened it up and put it all into my tin billy and boiled it up, made a sort of yeasty mixture out of it, which was probably useful sort of tucker. When I'd eaten the bird I made a soup of sorts by boiling some of the bones up as well.

I shot a pig another day, over the other side of the river, and brought it back to the camp in the dinghy. The wild pigs up in that country are a healthy lot on the whole, don't have as much disease as they do in some areas. All the same it's wise to inspect the carcass for parasites, things like that, and cook it well. Which I did. Pork made another bit of a change from beef.

As time went on I found that I was missing salt badly as well as sugar. And that was a worry, because I was getting cramps as a result. A bit ironical, after the hell of a struggle I'd had to try and get away from salt, on the river. The water back as far as the low falls is fresh to brackish; to get to really heavily salt water I would have had to go over the falls again . . . then wait for the next tide to return. Even then I don't know if salt water would have done any good, would probably have just made me vomit, and anyway I would have lost as much salt sweating getting downriver and back as I might have gained from salt water. I thought a shark might have some salt in its flesh. I don't know if they do, but as they live in salt water most of the time it was worth a try. I tied a piece of meat to a strip of greenhide as bait, and when a shark came in to get it, lured it close in to the bank and shot it. It didn't taste very salty, not when it was cooked, but at least it was another variation to the menu.

Cindy's leg was just about better. I'd been walking her round the camp a bit, exercising her gently, and at the end of four weeks I took the splint off. She was beginning to put her foot to the ground, and gradually getting better. After a couple of days, when I next took Bouncer out hunting, I let her come, too.

We had to go a fair way, a couple of miles from the camp, before we got onto cattle in an open area of tall grass. When I let them off the leash Bouncer took off after a cow, and she only galloped about twenty yards when she spun round on him, and he just ran around her because he wasn't game to grab hold of her by himself—he was still only a little dog. But when he saw me running up and the cow take off again he chased her the second time. That time the cow went about a hundred yards and chasing her that distance he got hot; had to work to keep after her, so got his blood up.

When she turned to charge him the second time he just kept running straight in and grabbed her by the bottom jaw, and didn't let go. He was no weight, so the cow kept spinning round trying to hook him but couldn't get at him. He had a really good grip, all four feet off the ground, going round and round in circles. I was able to race in and grab her by the tail and pull her down. It was the first time he'd pulled up a beast without assistance, so he was coming along well. But she was a poor old skinny cow, not worth killing, no meat on her at all, so I let her go.

When it was over, I found that Cindy wasn't there, hadn't caught up in the chase. I waited for her, called her for about half an hour, but she never came. I thought she had probably headed back to the camp, but when we got back, she wasn't there either.

All that night I hoped she would turn up, but she didn't, and I thought: "That's it, the dingoes have got her." All the same, I walked back in the direction we'd been hunting and called her again but just couldn't find her.

When I got back to the camp I let Bouncer off from being tied up to have a run around, and was just sitting, feeling pretty bad about losing the little white dog, when Bouncer suddenly raced off up the bank and started playing in a patch of long grass. I went up to have a look, and there she was, Cindy. Had probably been there all along, gone back to the camp after missing us in the hunt and hidden. She looked very down in the mouth and seemed to think she had done something terrible by being separated from us. I had to tell her she was a good dog and make a fuss of her before she cheered up and came back into the camp. I felt a good deal better too. The thought of having lost one of them had been pretty depressing. Those dogs were very important to me.

From then on I took both dogs with me hunting. Even though she was limping and couldn't always keep up in a chase, it was training for Cindy. Bouncer was coming on well, and once they were both able to work properly I felt we were going to be all right, even if I ran out of ammunition. Whenever we got close enough to a beast to pull it down without using the gun I would cut its throat, not waste a bullet.

6

Thoughts on the City and the Bush

I'd been there about five weeks when a light plane came over my way. Not close enough, though. I was a fair way from the camp when I heard it coming, just a drone in the distance, and ran like hell to try and get to the fire and pile on the green branches for a signal. But it was a hopeless try. By the time I galloped into the open near the camp I could see the plane, just a small speck over toward the gorge, and then it was gone, out of sight behind the hills. No amount of jumping up and down and yelling or making smoke signals was going to do any good; whoever it was had no idea I was there. It was a bit of a blow, listening to it fading away, but I thought that, well, if one had come over then maybe another would . . . one day. Or the same one come back by the same route. But it didn't.

I wasn't too happy at that stage. The cramps from the lack of salt were getting worse, affecting my hunting. And the lack of stamina from not having any sugar wasn't improving. I was still strong enough, could lift and carry as much as before, but had to take a spell more often. I wasn't exactly sick, but not exactly well, either. I was starting to worry about getting out, not that I doubted I would when the time came, but I began to think it would take longer than I'd anticipated. Was thinking I'd probably have to work to a billabong or some good place for game, rest there for a bit, and then go on to the next likely spot, and do the same. Not be able to do it all in one hit, and so take three weeks or more instead of the ten or twelve days I'd first thought. But I'd get out when the rains came, I was sure I could do it, if I took it easy.

I had to do something about the salt problem. In that climate, even in the dry season, you lose a lot of salt doing anything strenuous during the day. The nights and early mornings might be cool, but it gets hot once the sun's well up. The cattle were getting touchy, very toey, they knew something was up and that I was the cause. Nearly every hunt took me further and further out. Went right down to the gorge in the dinghy on the tide and got a beast down there one day, brought the meat back on the outgoing tide, but I didn't want to ruin that area entirely for hunting too early in the game. Keep it as a backstop. Away from the river I found I had to go as far as eight miles on one occasion, and you lose a lot of sweat, and salt, lugging a load of meat that distance. The only source of salt I could think of, apart from the shark, which was dubious, was blood. So I drank fresh blood after I'd cut a beast's throat. Did that a couple of times. It didn't taste too bad, warm, and, well, a bit salty, but I couldn't drink much of it. I think it did some good, probably not a lot, but it was better than nothing.

But none of this altered my attitude to the bush itself. If anything, I think I gained even more respect for it, and I still like it, and wouldn't want to live anywhere else but in the bush. I've always known it was capable of being a hard place, and I still know that. It's a hard place because, although other countries, like Africa for instance, have more predators, lions and bears and other gear that's dead-set dangerous (except that Australia's probably got more snakes than anywhere else) they also have a lot of other things that help man to survive—herds of deer and other game, all sorts of alternatives for food. It's the overall scarcity of the Australian bush that makes it hard. Food's there but it isn't easy to find.

I'm sure the Australian Aboriginals would have developed a different way of life if they had been on another continent. Take the Fitzmaurice River country. To the Aboriginal that would have been country of plenty, a rich country, but their idea of plenty, when it comes down to it, just meant that it was less hard than other places. Certainly the country gives you nothing. Bush nuts and fruits might be there, but never handed to you on a plate. And the native fauna, wallabies and kangaroos, are not all that plentiful, usually scattered and not in big mobs, and they're pretty flighty. Good eyesight, good hearing and sense of smell. Very alert and quick off the mark. It must have been hard for the Aboriginal before cattle were introduced, and I know if cattle hadn't been there I would have been in a lot of trouble. You couldn't say that the bush opposes man—it's not hostile, but it's indifferent, and life in it is always a bit precarious.

I think this affected the white Australian's attitude to life in general, for a long time. But the modern, urban Australian, and most of them are urban, has got so far removed from his country, history, and beginnings, that the influence is no longer there. Not so much, anyway. There are still remnants from generations before when the bush had a big influence on our development, our culture—identity if you like, but I think that's now gradually disappearing. One reason for the big gap between city and country.

It's very strange. If I go down to the city, and I've only done that a couple of times in my life; fair enough, it's all new to me, but I still have a very good idea of what a city is like, know what to expect. Some things are a bit strange, and it's all new and exciting; but by the same token, I have a very good idea of what I will find what I get there.

But urban people have no idea whatsoever of the outback, the wild country of Australia—the whole of the Top End, the North—they have no idea what it's like and can't even comprehend when it's explained to them. This is in spite of the recent awareness about conservation and the wilderness, and all that. It's good for them to use National Parks, get out into the country again, but it's still so removed from what I'd call the real Australia that still exists in the far North that there's really no comparison. At least going and camping in a Park or something is a step in the right direction, toward recognizing that Australia is their land and they've got to look after it, a step toward getting back to what the majority of Australia is all about, area-wise. The population is all urban, but the area is all bush except for thin strips on the coast.

And the bush makes the bushman have a different outlook, way of looking at life, especially about putting up with things. They tend to be very philosophical about life. They know things will constantly go wrong that they have no control over, they don't give in to them, but accept the fact that they have to work round things all the time. They have to come to terms with the land, and even in the bush some of this is being lost today. A lot of the old traditional ways are going. I don't just mean whether they use helicopters or horses for mustering, not just that, but the attitude to the cattle and the land. There are places where they can use a plane or a helicopter to muster but still handle cattle in the traditional manner where each beast is important, where the weaners are tailed—held in a mob for a couple of days and educated by men on horseback, so that they get used to being handled—where the mickeys are cut and branded and put in a bullock paddock. Where they combine the best of old and new methods.

The old-time stockman, using the old methods, was always in contact with the land, he loved the bush, understood it, and accepted the challenge to live in it. He slept on the ground—wherever he put down his swag was home to him, his possessions were few and yet he was in his own way quite comfortable. His relationship with the land and the cattle was a very personal one, every beast was considered important, work was very much on a man-to-beast basis. He knew the country intimately, which areas were being grazed too heavily, how many cattle could be got out of other areas without depleting the herd. It was a matter of coming to terms with the land, not fighting it, but somehow having some sort of devious control over it. Very hard work with horses but somehow a certain control was held, no matter how seemingly fragile.

When helicopter mustering is used without combining it with some of the old methods as well, it's bad news. If you tear into cattle with a helicopter, just racing them into a yard with a big scare racket, you lose that control. Calves get left behind when cows gallop too hard and fast, bulls get hot and bail up under trees, bullocks get overheated and die, a lot of beasts get damaged. It doesn't always happen like that, but it can and does. No doubt the numbers look good on paper to the board of directors—six or seven hundred head yarded in a day—but it's no good in the long run. Next year those cattle are as mad as march hares and the whole thing starts to get out of control. There's no doubt that helicopter mustering is a contributing factor to the number of wild bulls in the North today. There have always been a lot—it's a big country—but there are more now than ten or twelve years ago.

It's not just the money on paper thing, it's also a matter of the stations being able to get men who will come to grips with the land. The type of person is changing who comes to the North. Perhaps in the Depression years if a man went from the city to the Top End it might have looked a pretty good bed of roses, plenty of beef and damper, good mates and hard work. But a bloke from the city today would probably have a heart attack if chucked into the average stock camp and expected to rough it.

But if you can accept that way of life, it's the best way for the bush. It's a full commitment, a getting right down to basics, down to man and the environment he lives in. You are eking out your existence from the first order, straight from the land itself, so you are on a very honest relationship in your own life. You have to rely on yourself, not on other people. Sleeping on the ground and hard camp conditions are part of it, part of the commitment and attitude. You get to like it, and in the end you can get straight up out of a swag on the ground and go and hop on a rough horse and maybe take a buster and it's no problem, whereas if you had to drag yourself out from a soft bed in the homestead it would be harder, it would influence your outlook. It would no longer be right down there where the basics are.

And, I think, that is how you have to be if you want to really come to terms with this land. And that's what divides the old style bushman from the new; not age, or which generation they belong to, but the attitude they have, the degree of their commitment to the bush itself.

The thing is, bull catching's a hard game on blokes. A few of them get killed, that's inevitable in any job with a fairly high risk factor. But a lot of them die alcoholics, because there's an image to keep up. The old Australian boozer's image is multiplied when it's put in contact with the big bull catcher, who's got to drink gallons of the stuff or he's no good at all, see. So, if they get on the grog, then that impairs their judgment, impairs their work and ability. You only have to have one really bad prang—hit one big stump and wreck your vehicle—and you're buggered for the year. Even if that doesn't happen, a bloke on the booze doesn't maintain his gear properly, and so he starts to go downhill.

There was one bloke I knew, helluva good bloke he was, but the worst thing he ever did was start catching bulls. Because he labored under the image of being a bull catcher until he committed suicide at Fanny Bay, went and chucked himself over the cliff, the big jump there. He just labored under the image, no other description for it. Having been a bull catcher once he wouldn't look at any other job, and to be a bull catcher he had to drink mobs of grog and he wasn't good at drinking mobs of grog. Then he took up with a girl. I'm not saying she was no good, but she possibly wasn't the best choice for him. They got on okay for a while, then she decided the bush life wasn't for her, sleeping on the ground and eating rough tucker. Well, he could've said the girl was the most important thing, and tried a job in the city, or made a better camp, but he wouldn't change, and the girl shot through, and he chucked himself off the cliff. That was it. Finish of him and he was a good bloke.

Now, there's another bloke, Ralph Searle, who's got a very good base camp, 240 generator, caravan, everything there, and his wife, Sadie, lives out there and cooks for the camp. It's all very good. But that's the wrong image for a bull catcher, you're supposed to sleep on the ground and wake up and have rum for breakfast. Ralph's an exception, and a bloody good bull catcher, no worries about that, and he doesn't suffer from being an exception. Exceptions never do. But a lot of blokes can't see that.

The thing is, I think, that Ralph started catching fairly late in life, in his thirties, so he had himself, his own character, sorted out well beforehand. Whereas with young blokes going into it at an impressionable age, often their own characters get pushed to the back and the bull catcher's got to come to the front. So, I reckon, if you're going to avoid letting the image take over, you've got to be prepared to be a bit of an exception. And get by, somehow.

7

Memories in Loneliness

There was no doubt about having to get down to basics out on the Fitzmaurice; the layers of civilization, or whatever, couldn't be stripped down much further, that was for sure.

With the cattle getting harder to get near all the time, I couldn't risk any hampering, any noise. Even a pair of shorts can seem to catch on every twig, scratch through every patch of grass, when you're trying to be totally silent, taking several seconds to slide your foot forward on the next step, that kind of thing. So I chucked them off, and went hunting naked.

The days weren't all bad, even then, but went up and down. Some days I felt ratshit, depressed about getting weaker, worried . . . and lonely. The next day would be better if things seemed to look up. It all depended on how things went.

I missed a shot one day. That was bad. After hours getting onto cattle, then slowly stalking to get a good shot lined up, and miss, somehow. That was very bad. No second chance with the cattle off and away. And needing meat badly.

I shot the old bull who'd been hanging around near the camp, the one I'd kept in reserve. Not the best meat in the world, but meat, and that was the main thing. The kill wasn't far from the camp, maybe a hundred yards, and in the night the dingoes came howling in. In the stillness out beyond the campfire I could hear them snarling over the carcass, bones cracking as they crunched into them. Dingoes, kites, crows, ants and flies, the predators and scavengers of the bush, and part of the cycle of nature and of life. I was doing a lot of thinking, not just because I had the time, but because, even if only subconsciously, I probably wanted to sort things out in my mind, keep a grip on things. Thought about myself, and my life and where it was heading and why, and about life and the world in general.

There was religion, which I'd never thought about in terms of myself. Had more or less thought about it as a whole concept, other people and nations and sects, which didn't concern myself. I'd had what you'd call a fairly religious upbringing, been taken to church with my parents, Sunday school when ever possible, that kind of thing. But I rejected orthodox religion—and still do, can't swallow the whole bit as it is. The Bible as Gospel Truth, hellfire and if you don't go to church on Sunday you're not a Christian—there's too much there for me to accept, and if you're going to be religious in the orthodox way I don't think you can go halfway. The Bible is a fantastic book, the fact is that it still has some relevance although written so long ago, but has less and less relevance as the times and the world change. You've got to look for increasingly devious routes to get back to it, and I think that's wrong.

Thinking about that, I decided that I am religious, because I definitely believe that life is not self-made, the earth and planets and the whole universe. It all started somewhere, somehow.

But I don't think I can ask for anything, that it's a God that when you get into a tight fix you can pray to and he's going to say, "Oh yair, rightyo, mate, I'll get you out of a bit of a jam," and whammo there you are. That's not on the cards at all. But I still thank God or whatever or whoever it is, just for being alive and for the earth and the things of beauty it contains, and for the things I am able to experience. And you've got to include all sorts of things in that. You've even got to be grateful for pain in a way, because if you didn't have it you wouldn't know what it was to be without it. If you've never been sad, then being happy means nothing. The whole thing revolves around that—even good and evil.

I can't think of the universe, the earth, and the environment as being anything but good, to be appreciated, and the force behind it, the greater magnitude of consciousness, whatever it is, as a force for good. But people? Unfortunately, people seem to have the biggest mobs of evil in them—myself included in lots of ways. Call it the fault of human nature. People seem hell-bent on destroying our world, and each other. We're a very murderous species, kill each other in countless thousands at different times, can never get together to agree on any policy for the world on which we live. And it's very sad. People constantly hurt each other, and you can bet your bottom dollar if you are hurt personally it is usually by other people or something man-made.

But that view of the human race is only negative if you look at it one way. If you look at it from the other side of the argument, but with the same view—that even the painful or bad has a purpose—then you can be positive about it. Then you say, all right, human nature's got basic evil in it, but there are plenty of people who are very nice in every way, that there is good in people, and that good is due to individual effort. It's within everyone's power to be good and this is a very positive thing. It means you can be an individual, that being good takes an effort, and that increases its value. If everyone was just good it wouldn't mean so much. So if you look at it that way it's a very positive attitude.

But I don't think orthodox religion has much to do with it.

That God or Jesus Christ will make us good. I don't think Jesus
Christ has a hope in hell of making some of us good. I don't
think he's got a hope of making any of us good. I think it's up
to us. Maybe religion should have brought the standards of
people up, but unfortunately it's been abused from the start,
right from the start they've been killing people in the name of
religion—holy wars and that. You can't preach one thing and
do another. No way you can justify killing thousands of people in the name of religion. "Love thy Neighbor" and then go
out and kill a few thousand. But religion's always been like that.
It tends to attract fanatics, and they're dangerous people.

I try never to think about politics, it's the dirtiest business
in the world. But I did think a bit about Watergate and all the
fuss about that. The whole trouble with following the media
is that you never know what's going on. You can only believe
what you're told, which is bugger-all in my opinion. Which is
a real sad state of affairs. But, I thought, ah well, old Nixon's
got himself into a bit of trouble. Not because he's a cheat or a
liar, it's just that he's been silly enough to get caught. The rest
of them are just the same, they've just got this aura of respect-
ability draped around their shoulders. Nixon didn't even look
like a President, so he never had a hope, right from the start.
Take the Kennedys and their whole "good men" style. They
could have got away with murdering their grandmother. Then
you come to old Richard Nixon, an ugly-looking turnout, he
never had a chance. He was a bit of a bungler from the start,
probably stepped on a few toes, so they decided to crucify him.
I thought, well, that's a bit of a pity. After all, he wasn't any
worse than the others, it was just that they decided they'd catch
him. All that business about bugging rooms and apartments,
you can't tell me it didn't go on all the time. Probably still does.
All just covered up a bit better. Nixon was roped in due to a
third-rate bungle up of a third-rate burglary. Nothing fright-

fully dramatic like selling secrets to the Russians for millions of dollars, nothing like that, but it was the lynch rope that got him hung.

The trouble with politicians is the way they get elected, through the gift of the gab. They get up there in front of everybody and proceed to lie blatantly and the one who makes the most convincing job of it gets elected. That's a terrible way to hire the men who are going to run your nation. They get up there and say, "We shall," they don't say, "We might" or "We could" or "We'll try" but: "We *shall* do this and *shall* do that. Stop unemployment, lower the rate of inflation, bring so many millions of dollars into the country, help the cattle man, help the sheep man, help the union man, the employers *and* the employees. All at once." And that's just got to be the most blatant form of lying you've ever come across, in front of everybody like that. When time has proved over and over again that this just doesn't happen. I don't care what Party it is, they're all the same, and I don't know how people can be silly enough to believe the lies politicians tell them, and believe in them enough to actually fight over them.

Maybe people like to be told lies. It's part of our whole way of life, fraud and deception, with advertising promising all sorts of things. We'll watch five different soap commercials on TV all saying theirs is the best, and believe every one of them. Something's wrong somewhere.

People seem to need a crutch, something to believe in, but I don't think religion or politics or the media, all the heroes and heroines of film and TV and the entertainment industry, I don't think any of these is the answer.

It just comes back to individualism, that's the only way I can see it. There's a terrific potential in people to be worthwhile individuals. And it's up to them, to all of us, to work toward that. We've got to get back to the idea that we're all responsible for our own actions, not somebody or something else. I don't mean we should turn a blind eye to what's going on around us, nothing is worse than finding someone wants help, needs help, and you haven't noticed. But we shouldn't go out of our way to interfere with other people's lives, which the human race tends to do, constantly.

Maybe a part of all this thinking things out, sort of discussion with myself, was because I had a subconscious feeling I wasn't going to get out of there for a long, long time, or not at all. I don't know. It certainly wasn't a conscious thought, because I always believed that I would get out eventually, however long it took me.

And a sense of identity is a strange thing. With no one to talk to, you begin to lose your feeling of who you are. It's probably like the thing about time: with nothing to relate time to, it would be like living in a vacuum, so keeping track of days became important. In the same kind of way a mirror is about the last thing I'd ever want, absolutely. But out on the Fitzmaurice, I wanted a mirror. It was an identity-type thing, to see who I was, what I looked like. Partly just to see a human face, but more to check on myself. One of the lids from a milk tin, cleaned and rubbed up a bit, gave a reflection of sorts. Pretty ratshit and distorted, but it was a reflection of a face. I didn't get to the stage of talking to it, didn't get to that stage. And the dogs weren't talking back—not yet anyway. So I wasn't going mad.

But I was lonely. I wasn't afraid of the bush, didn't think it a terrible thing to be where I was—in fact, it's a beautiful area. But getting weaker, which I was doing, gradually, was a worry. And I was lonely. I wanted someone to talk to, discuss things with, have a yarn to, especially some of the old bushmen I'd known, the real old-timers.

I remembered the two old fellers, the Gorlick brothers, old

Tom and Jim, who'd been timber cutters, and they had a dirt-floored hut on one of the Forestry leases, one of the blocks my father took over. Old Jim only had one hand, he'd lost the other dynamiting fish when he was very young, and old Tom had something wrong with him too, an injury from an ax. When they heard someone had taken over the lease, they thought they'd have to leave, were quite resigned to it. When the Old Man went out to see them, they were packing up, ready to go. My father couldn't just tell them to stay, that'd be charity, they wouldn't have that, so he told them he needed them to stay on as caretakers. That was all right, they thought it was Christmas, and moved back into their little dirt hut. They were in their eighties then, and died when I was about fourteen, but I remember the way they had of putting things, like if a bit of country was hard country, they'd say: "Aw, she's bad, that end of the place. Saw a bandicoot with a cut lunch round his neck out there." The thing is, those old fellers were happy spending the rest of their days in a little dirt hut in the bush. They liked it, it was their home, their way of life. If some do-gooder had come along and shoved the poor old buggers in a nice clean home, that would have been the dead finish of them.

I would have liked very much to have a yarn with my parents, sit down and talk with my father about the things we had in common, the work we did, and remember things that had happened, have a bit of a laugh.

There was one thing the Old Man couldn't stand, and that was anyone criticizing his horses. You could sling off at anything else, say anything you liked about his kids or about him, and he wouldn't care, but not his horses. As kids we'd take great delight in getting a rise out of him. We'd be riding along and one of us would say: "That mare the old feller's riding, she's a bit long in the neck, eh? What do you reckon?" And the other one would have a think and then say: "Ah, dunno about long in the neck. Looks more like short in the back to me." And sure enough, father would get red in the face and start spluttering and we'd be off—take to the scrub.

Well, if we could have sat down and had a yarn, I thought, there'd be a few laughs at my expense, too.

Like the time he and I were out after cattle in the Black Snake country. Very rough and rugged, steep country and a lot of cattle, all sorts. All pretty wild, and we'd been having a very good run after one mob, throwing them one by one. In fact, had cattle tied up everywhere, a helluva good morning. We generally had two bull-straps, carried across the chest, one round the waist and one round the horse's neck, and that generally did you. Well, we'd used up all our straps, plus one rein each (tying the other ribbon to the bit to make a short rein), and I'd used up one stirrup leather and the belt I had round my jeans.

There were two beasts left, a cow and a big mickey, and we caught up with them on a bit of a flat. The old feller says: "You take the mickey and I'll take the cow," and off he went, sitting in on the cow, which went off to the left, and I took off after the mickey which went off to the right. You lose sight of each other very quickly in that sort of timbered country which is full of ridges and gulleys. I galloped after the mickey, got him pumped out pretty well, stepped off my horse and grabbed him. Threw him, and then with his tail twisted back and still hanging onto it to keep him down, sat on him—because I had to wait for the old feller to come back with something to tie this mickey up with.

I wasn't watching what I was doing, wasn't holding him right. He was having a big breather, lying there, got his wind back, gave a couple of kicks, and was up on his feet and off. I still had the end of his tail, but he was going at a fair pace. I was touching the ground every few yards—big long long strides— and my jeans are a couple of sizes too big for me, I can feel them slipping down. Running along like that, only barely keeping my feet, I couldn't pull them up. They got too far down, the old stride shortened a bit and over I went, klunk. So I was getting dragged along with my jeans right down over my boots, when the mickey decides, bugger this, he's going to spin and hook. So round he spun, and I can't get up because I'm having a bit of trouble, see. But while the front end of him was trying to get at me, I was being dragged away because I still had hold of his tail. He stood on my boots, one of them was pulled off by his front feet, but I was still being dragged away. Eventually got to my feet, but could hardly keep there, with the jeans about my ankles only letting me take six-inch steps, and I can't get round him fast enough to pull him down. And it's getting a bit desperate because he's getting fresher and fresher and I'm getting tireder. So round and round we went, him getting fresher and me getting tireder. I thought, it's no good, I'm just going to have to get to a tree. So when he pulled me off my feet again I just lay there, and he was hooking and dragging this way and that until we finally worked our way over to some overgrown saplings. Soon as I got near one I let go his tail and grabbed the sapling and stood up very fast behind it.

Now the mickey spun round and of course without me on his tail he could really concentrate on what he was doing. I had the tree between me and him, but it was still a bit of a problem, because those jeans were still impeding me and I was only just keeping ahead of him around the tree, dodging one side to the other. He was starting to bump me on the odd occasion, with the side of his horn or his neck as he tried to get at me round the tree, and he was giving that sapling a fair pushing, too.

All the time, in the back of my mind, I'm thinking: "The old feller's got to get here soon. He can't be far away. He must be here in a minute." And around the tree we go. Then I become conscious of a half-moaning noise behind me, and when I get round the other side, so I can look that way, I can see what it is. There's father. And he's laughing that much he's crying, he's lying down on the old horse's neck, pulling handfuls of mane out and punching the horse. Laughing his guts out. Of course I did my block: 'Get off that damn horse and come over here, you old bastard.' And the more I yelled the more he laughed. The mickey eventually got sick of the whole thing and took off. Just as well, the Old Man was laughing that much he was useless. Nearly fell off his horse for laughing.

Moral: don't get caught with your pants down.

Don't know if there's a moral in the next incident. There was a bit of a concert in town, years ago, local talent kind of thing. Anyone who could play the guitar, sing, recite a bit of poetry, anything, could get up on stage and have a bash at it. There was one old character who got up with a poem he'd written, which wasn't the best poetry in the world, and to make matters worse he had a lisp. Amongst other things this old bloke was, according to him, a "piano pruner." He was too, could "prune" pianos real well. But somebody in the crowd, halfway through his poem, yells out: "Why don't you go back to your piano pruning, eh?" He took offense at this, got all hot and flustered, threw the microphone down and yelled back: "I can truth up a thcrub bull in the buth and I can truth you too." Jumped off the stage and into this other bloke, hammered hell out of him, got him down on the floor, and choked him properly. That done, he crawled back up onto the stage, picked up the microphone, and carried on with his poem. Everyone clapped like mad, of course, weren't game to do otherwise.

If there's a moral in all that it's probably that it's wiser to keep your opinions to yourself.

Part Four

THE RESCUE

Previous page: *Luke McCall, one of Rod's rescuers*
Photo by Jan Kenny, © Rachel Percy

The Wild

I have flouted the wild,
I have followed her lure,
Fearless, familiar, alone;
Yet the end is near,
And the day will come,
When I shall be overthrown.

I have taunted the wild,
I have swum in her streams;
Following her mountains along.
Winning is sweet,
But the victory is short;
For the life of a man isn't long.

I have baited the wild,
Yet my bones shall lie hid,
And their rotting make wild flowers grow;
For you can change enemy
And friend into one,
And this is the power of my foe.

I have parried and struck
At your guarded might
And stepped 'neath your hardest blows;
Yet you will win,
With your time and stealth,
And mine be the eyes that close.

1

Horse Bells

The tide was coming in, and bringing something with it. At first it was just a distant, indeterminate sort of sound, but something different from anything I'd been hearing. It got louder. A definite clunking, banging metallic kind of noise. Metal! A boat? I raced down the bank to see who or what it was. Couldn't see anything, and what the hell a boat could be doing coming up the Fitzmaurice I had no idea, but—well, anything is possible. Started hurrying toward the nearest bend, and heard a couple more bangs and thumps; whatever was making the noise was still coming up the river. I tried not to be too hopeful, not get too excited. The noise got closer.

And there it was. An empty forty-four gallon drum, rolling about in the tide, crashing and bashing itself against the banks and bits of driftwood. Just an empty oil drum. Christ knows where it had come from.

It was a disappointment, no doubt about that. Watching that drum slowly rolling past on its way upstream, just another bit of rubbish. As a symbol of civilization it was, I suppose, fairly appropriate, but rather depressing. It didn't come back on the turn of the tide. Must have got stuck somewhere, or final-ly sank.

I knew all along that there wasn't going to be any rescue party coming up the river. The two months would soon be up, and then, once I was overdue back at Kununurra, Lor-raine would probably make some inquiries, draw a blank, and raise the alarm. But it wouldn't do me any good. Even if someone did find my vehicle back on the Victoria, I was a hell of a long way from there. No one was likely to go looking up the Fitzmaurice, that was for sure. No. They'd check out the Victoria River area, maybe find some trace of my boat, and reckon I'd drowned. That'd be it. Which would cause a few people, like my parents, to get upset, something I'd rather didn't happen. I never write letters—think I'd written once the year before—so they work on the theory that no news is good news.

In the meantime, I was sitting there while everyone else was going about their business. They didn't think anything was the matter. Everything goes on without you, whether you're there or not. It makes no difference, really.

I thought of all the other people who'd been stranded in the same way. There must have been a lot of people over the years, and even at the very same time, all over the world, stranded on an island or something, and not able to get in contact with other people. Some of them might have been stranded for years, perhaps even died without anyone knowing about them, even to this day. These things have a very limited projection. Even when someone dies under normal circumstances, who knows but his immediate friends? Unless he happens to be a person of some notoriety, and then he has a last burst of glory in the news for a week. Then everyone forgets straightaway.

I wasn't feeling at all good at this stage but, as usual, things weren't all bad. I'd shot a cow. A big fat cow, a bit too much for the little dogs to try and pull down at that stage of their progress. A beautiful big fat barren cow, one of the fattest I've ever seen. Well worth the extravagance of a bullet. So I had really good meat in the camp.

I seemed to be going up and down every day by now. A good day, then a bad one. Up and down.

A few days later I woke up late. The sun was well up, it must have been about eight in the morning. I'd slept in, probably because I wasn't feeling very well, and woke up all hot and sweaty. Thought, "Bugger that," because I had to go hunting again. I'd smelled the rib bones hanging up the night before, and reckoned I'd get one more feed off them before I had to bush the rest—throw them out. So I crawled out of the swag, took off my jeans and jacket, dragged on the old black shorts, built the fire up a bit, and sat down to sharpen my knives before I went out.

I was just sitting there, sharpening a knife on the stone, slowly swishing it back and forth, and I was thinking to myself: "Horse bells." That was all, just kept sharpening my knife and kept thinking "Horse bells," and about how they're sort of synonymous with the bush. Then all of a sudden it clicked: "It *is* horse bells!" It just hadn't registered, hadn't sunk in. Then I thought: "No, no, it's not." And I reckoned it was something hung up somewhere, maybe the bullet belt tapping against the scope of my rifle, hanging in the tree. Something like that making that tinny noise. Looked around, didn't get up, just looked round. There wasn't a breeze, nothing was moving.

And I heard horse bells again. Thought: "It *must* be horse bells." So I got up and went to the edge of the river and listened, because I wasn't sure whether the sound was coming from across the river or if it was an echo thrown back from the big ridge on the other side. The sound was definitely on the other side, and then I saw a wallaby go shooting up the

ridge beyond the tall grass. Something over there had fright-
ened it. Now I got a glimpse of something in the grass, a
movement, and something—it could have been a hat—going
along. Then it had gone.

I gave a yell and raced for the dinghy. Rowing like mad across
the river I thought: "It's definitely horse bells. It's got to be
horse bells. There's definitely something over there. Either that
or I've gone round the bend. Gone mad. Troppo." I had to
find out. Quick.

Got to the far side, hitched the boat to a tree root, and
scrambled up the high bank. Then had to stop and listen. The
bells had moved on, were heading upriver, and I went after
them, trying to keep them within earshot. Cut the horse tracks
and followed those as fast as possible. The long grass was neck
high along there, hadn't had a fire through it for years, and I
was pushing and shoving and trying to run through it. Gave a
couple of yells, and kept on going. Then, just up ahead, I saw
a hat. Just a big dark hat above the tall grass. And raced for
that. Gave another shout, a bit of a cooee . . . and got a cooee
back. The hat sort of spun round and waited as I pushed my
way through the grass toward it.

And there was this bloke, riding a mule. A whitefellow,
dressed in black, with a blue bandana scarf, his hat pushed back
a bit, white hair and beard, and his mouth open.

I said: "G'day."

He said: "Where'd you come from, how'd you get here?"

I told him I'd had a bit of bad luck, that my boat had tipped
over, and he asked me how long I had been there, and I told
him I wasn't sure for certain, but about seven weeks.

He said: "It's Friday today. Did you know what day it is?"

And I said: "No. I never know what day it is."

Then he said he was Luke McCall, and I told him my name
and we shook hands, and he said they were from Palumpa sta-

tion, over a hundred miles away. There was a blackfellow, an old fellow, waiting up ahead, looking back, very curious, and Luke sung over to him: "Hey, Raphael, get Big Rupert. Tell Big Rupert there's a whitefellow here."

I waited, and wondered a bit while Raphael and Big Rupert rode up. In most camps, Luke McCall would be the boss, but the way he sung out for Big Rupert to be told what was going on sounded like it was a different kind of setup. I didn't realize then that the country we were on was part of Palumpa, a fairly new Aboriginal station, run by an Aboriginal Council—like a board of directors—and that Rupert was the Head, so more or less the owner, or principal owner. And Luke McCall was their cattle manager.

Anyway, Raphael, Big Rupert, and another younger black-fellow, Christopher, rode up, all looking a bit surprised, but not letting on too much. Luke McCall told Big Rupert who I was, we were all introduced and had a bit of a yarn, with me telling them how I'd had the accident and about having to come up the river for fresh water, that kind of thing. Then Luke said they didn't have much in the tucker-bags, just a bit of flour and sugar and so on, but how about me joining them for din-ner camp? And did I have any tucker? I told them all I had was some meat, a set of rib bones, but that was good because they were right out of beef, with no cattle over that side, and were pretty hungry too.

Luke asked Big Rupert where the crossing was, where they were going to stop for dinner camp (lunch), and Rupert told him just a little bit further, up near the bend. That was just up from my camp, so we fixed it that I'd go back and get the rib bones and join them there. They rode off to catch up with the rest of their horse plant that was spreading out a bit, and I heard Luke laughing, saying to Rupert: "Thought I was going bonkers when that feller popped out of the grass behind me!"

It must have been a bit of a shock. A skinny white feller, all hair and whiskers, looking pretty wild and wearing just a pair of old black footy shorts, springing on him out of nowhere.

Back at my camp, it started to sink in, that I'd been rescued, would be getting out of there. It was such a tremendous stroke of luck, them coming along like that. A bit hard to believe, really.

I tore up the bank to the dogs, grabbed them and hugged them, rolled them around and pulled their ears, told them we were going home: "Home, how about that?" But the foolish hounds just sat and grinned at me. Hadn't a clue.

By the time I'd rowed up to the crossing the others were waiting on the bank, looking out for me, and helped pull the boat in, and we all climbed up to the top bank. They had a fire going, and the camp all set up. Even though it was just a dinner camp they'd unsaddled all the pack and riding horses, and everything was put down very neat and tidy. The horses, about eighteen of them, were spread out having a bit of a feed and a spell, the bells clinking away as they moved about. It was like getting home, that sound, and that kind of scene, a packsaddle camp, all the gear, and stockmen round a fire with the billy boiling for a drink of tea.

Luke asked me what I was hungry for, what I wanted most, and I said: "Sugar, I need sugar bad. And flour and salt." So he opened up one of the milk tins they had tucker packed in and gave me a lump of sugar, a real big lump as big as your fist. We cooked and ate the rib bones. I had a real good sprinkling of salt on mine, and a bit more on my hand, just licked it from the palm of my hand.

And we all had a bit of a yarn. It wasn't hard talking to them, even after being by myself for such a long time, because we were the same sort of people. Talked about the country, horses, cattle, the things we all knew and understood. Well, the Aborigines didn't say much at first, let Luke do most of the talking, just sat and listened. They asked me how I'd got the meat, how I'd killed the cow, and I told them I had a big gun, and they reckoned it was a very good fat cow. Which it was. We had a cup of tea, and Luke told me to help myself, to come over to the fire and help myself, because I'd been sitting under a tree a little bit away. A bushman's fire is like your living room in town, you don't just go up and squat down by someone's fire any more than you'd walk into someone's sitting room without being invited in.

I went over and poured tea out of the billy into a pannikin, got powdered milk and sugar out of the tins, put the lids back, and was taking a drink when I noticed Luke giving me a pretty dirty look. I thought: "Something's up, I've done something wrong. Didn't put the wet spoon back in the sugar. Didn't leave the lids off. So what is it?" Then I realized that the tins were all lined up in a row, and I'd pushed one of them a bit off center. I pushed it back into line, and put the spoon across the top, the way I'd found it.

Luke gave a bit of a grin, and that was it. He's a very tidy man, Luke McCall, keeps everything in camp just so. Which is fair enough, we all have out own ways of coping with life in the bush. Our own rules, disciplines if you like, which help us to survive out there. He's a big man, and although he's got white hair, he's not more than about fifty, has clear blue eyes and very white teeth, talks very fast. Always wears black when he's out in the bush, always wears a red or blue bandana, and, like most people in the country, has a nickname . . . or two. He's known as The Black Prince or The Iron Man.

After a bit the Aborigines started asking a few questions, joined in the talking.

Old Raphael, who's a little thin fellow, very shy, doesn't

speak much English at all, so—they were all sitting in a row—he'd ask Big Rupert something, and then Big Rupert would ask Luke, and Luke would ask me. The answer would go back the same way. Big Rupert is a very tall, good-looking strong man, has a definite air of authority about him. He speaks good English, but in that soft Aboriginal voice.

Young Christopher is just a young feller who didn't say much at all, and when he did it was in the most deadpan voice you ever heard. Luke reckons you could be standing next to a king brown snake and Christopher would still use the same tone of voice to inform you of the fact.

Raphael wanted to know if I'd found any yams while I was there, and I said no I hadn't, well, none to speak of. They told me that it was very good yam country, that in the old days the Fitzmaurice used to be called the Country of the Long Yams. That the tribes used to go there to collect them and pretty well live on them at certain times. If I'd found one of those it would have done me for about a week, the Long Yam is about as long and as thick as your arm, very starchy, while the ordinary small yam is more like the sweet potato.

Both Big Rupert and Raphael were Fitzmaurice people. Raphael had been born there; I'm not sure about Big Rupert, but he lived there as a boy, when it was still tribal country. And Raphael had been there in the days of the Aboriginal outlaw, Nemarluk, who used to escape from the police over into the wild country beyond the Fitzmaurice. The crossing where we were was known as Policeman's Crossing, they told me, because that's where Nemarluk used to dash over the river. All that was in the mid 1930s. Soon after when the mission was started at Port Keats, the tribespeople moved over there.

I was told a bit more about Palumpa; that the homestead was about 140 miles to the North and that they had ridden over the bad ranges to the Fitzmaurice for a couple of reasons.

One was that Rupert and Raphael wanted to have a look at their old country again, and also they were hoping to check out on a place called Cooliman Creek, which they thought might be good cattle country. Raphael hadn't been back in that area for many many years, but still remembered the landmarks well. Big Rupert had worked on Bradshaw for four years, and he had been with the last mustering plant sent in to try and get some of the cattle out of the Fitzmaurice country, about seven years before. So he had been back in the area. I asked them about a big crocodile in the gorge, but although they both said there were plenty of big alligators (crocodiles) in the river, neither of them had seen a very very big one, so he must have moved there only in comparatively recent years. (Later, when I met Dick Gill from Bradshaw, he knew of the big old crocodile, had seen him from the air, even taken an aerial photograph of him on a bank near some grazing cattle. Said he made the cattle look like rabbits.)

After we'd had a good yarn, it was time for them to push off further upriver, to try and get to Cooliman Creek. Luke offered to turn back straightaway, get me to Palumpa as soon as possible, but I said another couple of days made no difference to me. So we arranged that they'd pick me up on the way back, probably in two or three days. That was all right.

Luke gave me some sugar, some treacle, coffee, and a johnny cake (small damper). Didn't have much left in their packs of anything. Then they saddled up and moved off, the jingling of the horse bells fading into the bush. I rowed back to my camp, and that didn't bother me at all, being left alone again. I knew they'd be back.

2

Making Tracks

That night, when the curlews called out on the flat and then old bulls started rumbling and grumbling in the distance, working themselves up to enough rage and indignation to start shrieking and bellowing, I just sat up by the fire and listened. I was getting out, going home. Soon there'd be no one to hear them. They'd have their bit of wilderness to themselves again.

It turned out to be sooner than I expected. The next day, still fairly early, I heard those horse bells again, went down to the river, and got a cooee from the far bank. So I threw everything into the dinghy—the dogs, my swag, rifle and that, the greenhide rope, and the crocodile head I'd kept—and rowed across.

Luke met me and explained that they had been forced to turn back up in the gorge. Too much rain-forest-type dense growth, and they couldn't get the horses through. They'd camped the night up there, watered the horses, had a look around, and then come back. They'd spend that night at Policeman's Crossing, and push off in the morning. The horses were getting tired, they were out of tucker, just about. It was time they headed for home.

The next morning the few things I had went into one of the packs, with the crocodile head in a corn bag tied on top. We reckoned we'd have to change the big brown pack horses's name, from Slippery to Crocodile. I took two blankets out of the swag and folded them, Indian style, over the back of Cooney, the old bay horse I was to ride. They had no spare saddles, so I had to ride bareback. The blankets made it a bit more comfortable.

Luke wondered how the puppy dogs would travel, but I said I thought they'd trot along all right. Cindy was still limping badly, so I was a bit concerned about how she'd go. Bouncer was as fit as a flea, no worries about him. Rupert, Raphael, and young Chris got a lot of amusement out of old Bouncer. He wasn't used to people, only me, and was very snooty, very aloof. Wouldn't talk to them, just stuck his nose in the air and looked away. Aborigines make a great fuss of their dogs, are used to them being friendly, and the young ones playful, so Bouncer acting so superior was a great joke.

The little dinghy had to be left, of course. No doubt it got swept away during the next Wet, could be anywhere now. Pity about that.

I knew I was in for a fairly stiff few days. A very long ride ahead of us, and not in the best of condition for tackling it. It was going to take about six days to get out, get back to Palumpa. But as Luke remarked, "Can't leave you here, eh?"

We only went a few miles that first day, which was a good thing as far as I was concerned. Not having been on a horse for months, and riding bareback, it wasn't the greatest. We swung away from the river, going sort of parallel with it, but at an angle, making for a little freshwater creek about ten miles out. Camped there for the rest of the day while Big Rupert and the others went hunting for meat, but didn't have any luck. So it was johnny cakes for tea that night, with a bit of treacle.

As everything came off the pack horses it was put down me-
thodically. Packs all in a row. Straps rolled and placed beside
each packsaddle, with the right bridle and blanket. Riding
saddles were hung up on branches, with their saddle blankets
and bridles. There's sloppy camps and neat, tidy ones. This
was one of the neatest, most efficient camps I've come across.
It's worth the trouble. Saddling up in the morning, there's
no running around, looking in the dirt for lost surcingles
and things. There were three packsaddles, one had the can-
teens hooked on it—tin water containers, which were filled
up whenever possible. The swags were carried across the tops
of the packs. Everyone travels light in a packhorse camp, no
extra gear at all; what can't go in a man's swag gets carried in
his saddlebag.

Old Raphael had a tin of baby powder, large economy size,
in his saddlebag. Each horse got a good dusting of powder over
its back after being unsaddled, to help prevent sore backs. The
horses were let loose to feed around, most with hobbles on.
Hobbles are two straps which go round the front fetlocks,
connected by a swivel chain. A hobbled horse can move around,
but, in theory, can't get up much of a pace. In practice a smart
horse soon learns how to hop along with both feet together,
and can move fast if it wants to. But good quiet horses don't
usually wander too far, and with the little horse bells round
their necks, it doesn't take long to find them. These were a
colorful mob, grays, chestnuts, bays, browns, and a lot of
"paints"—mixed color horses, skewbald and piebald. And the
mule, whose name is Fritter.

We always had two fires: one for the whitefellows, one for
the blackfellows. People who don't know about how things are
done in the bush get upset if they're told this. Think it's racist
or something. It isn't. It's privacy. When you're working and
camping together, all the time, your fire is your bit of private

territory. They weren't far apart, just a few yards, say five or six. For one thing, the Aborigines like to talk in their own language round the campfire, and it wouldn't be polite to do that with a whitefellow there, too. The same thing applies round a whitefellow's fire. Each group can do what they like in their own section of the camp. Luke being so very, very tidy, he reckoned he'd drive the other blokes mad if they all camped by the same fire. If anyone wanted a yarn, or to check up on something, they'd go over to the other blokes' fire, and be asked to sit down, the same as visiting your neighbor's house. It makes sense if you think about it.

The second day was another short one, taking us to the foot of the ranges, ready for the next stage, a long haul up the big jump-up and over into a hidden valley beyond. We camped at a spring not far from the big dirty creek I'd wondered about when I first went up the river. Was told it was a good thing I'd decided not to go up that creek. It stops short in the hills, is salt all the way, and has very steep high banks. Luke reckoned anyone going up it would have trouble getting out, would have been swept back with the tide, and Rupert and Raphael said it was a very bad creek, full of big cheeky "alligators"— they were careful to keep their horses well away from it.

There was a big boab near the camp, and we left our initials and the date carved in the trunk. The 27th of June, 1977. With no meat we cooked fresh johnny cakes in the ashes that night.

I wasn't feeling too good, very weak and giddy, throwing up. Couldn't eat much. Maybe it was the change in diet—after living on meat alone, going onto flour and sugar. And not having a hat. That was bad. Riding out in the sun wasn't the same as walking around in the bush, where you can keep in the shade a bit. On a horse you get the full belt of the sun the whole time. It made me feel crook. And maybe everything was starting to catch up with me, I don't know. I was just feeling bad. Crawled off to my swag early. Then Luke came over and asked how I was, did I have a touch of the sun? He had a spare hat in his swag which he could lend me, if I'd like it.

The hat was good the next day, because the ride was a very long one, starting at sunup. The only way up the big jump-up was a very faint old trail; a pad, which they called the Old Blackfellow Trail, used by the tribes in the old days, but no one had been over it for a long, long time. Raphael could still follow it, still knew it, even though it was probably over thirty years since he'd left the Fitzmaurice.

The horses all strung out Indian file, we plodded up and up, leading our riding horses most of the way. The narrow pad wound up the steep slope to a bit of a razor-back ridge, and then went up again for a second stage. A lot of rocks and loose boulders kept slipping and rolling to the bottom.

At the top, another narrow ridge, we could see right back over all the way we'd come, the flanking ranges, and the Fitzmaurice Valley away toward the horizon, the river just a gleam of reflected light winding through it.

Luke asked how I'd like to try walking it, try staggering through that on foot, and not knowing where to go. I said: "no way, thanks." It was a fairly formidable sort of view. Very hot and dry and altogether inhospitable. Even early in the morning the sun in the big blue sky sent heat bouncing back off the bare earth and rocks of the jump-up.

One good thing, the dogs were keeping up well, even Cindy, who was hopping along on three legs most of the way.

From the high ridge the pad wound down a very sharp descent, into a deep hollow, which Rupert said was Frog Hollow. There was a patch of quite thick rain forest down there, where Rupert found some "cabbage"—chopped the heart out of a grass tree. So we stopped for dinner camp, had a feed, and spelled the horses a bit, then went up out of the hollow, another steep climb, through a gorge they called Black Cockatoo, and from there down into the Valley.

3

Another Narrow Escape

The Majallindi Valley! I'd heard a lot about it. "Wait 'till you see the Valley . . . the big hidden Valley. We'll get a killer in the Valley, no trouble at all." But it was still a surprise to come down out of that barren range and find we were riding into a great, big, beautiful valley. Mostly flat plain, good rich grass country, looking a picture, and absolutely cut off from the rest of the world. It's about thirty or forty miles long, walled in by ranges on three sides, an almost uncrossable barrier, while, away on out left, it ran into marshes that eventually became salt pans down toward the "false mouth" that runs off the Fitzmaurice River. So that's where I'd have ended up, if I'd taken the false mouth by mistake, right at the beginning. I'd have bogged down in the marshes and salt pans. Definitely cactus.

But the Valley itself is something else, a pastoral paradise, grazed by wild cattle and brumbies which have never seen a man in their lives, most of them. Quite a big mob of buffalo, too. There's just one thing. With no control the Valley is in danger of being over-grazed in the near future, and Luke thinks that they will most likely have to go in soon and blow out some of the stock, shoot them to bring the numbers down.

Evidently the cattle and horses are all descended from some which had been taken in there many years ago. When the Mission at Port Keats was first starting up, the Aborigines told the missionaries about their big valley hidden in the ranges, and so some of them were sent to lead a quiet bull, a cow, a stallion and a mare over the range and release them in the Valley. Since then the numbers have bred up into big mobs, but none have ever been got out again. Very few white men have ever been into the Valley, only one or two that we know of apart from Luke and myself, and it has rarely been visited even by the Aborigines themselves over recent years.

One of these days the Palumpa people will work out a way to get stock out of the Valley, make a road of some kind, something, because it is the best land they have on the whole station. But before that they will probably have to go in and cut the numbers down, to save the land. The buffalo most likely got in by coming around through the coastal swamps and marshes. However they did it, they're there now.

We got a killer easily, which was good. Meat in the camp again. Then, a bit later, one of the Aborigines, I think it was Big Rupert, said how much he liked the pouch I'd made out of the bull's scrotum, so I said I'd make him one. Which was a bit rash, as it turned out.

I wasn't feeling too bad at the time, so left the others with the horses, and walked off toward a big old bull in the distance. I'd get up on him better on foot, but the trouble was, the wind was blowing the wrong way. I had to swing right out, and by the time I'd walked a long way down wind, and then a long way across the big open treeless plain, and could come up on him, I wasn't feeling too strong. Was starting to feel sick. Was out on the open plain, about thirty yards from this big scrub bull, and all of a sudden he realized I was there. At that moment I got giddy, sick, with everything spinning round, and I missed the first shot. Fired again and hit him on the point of the nose. He put his head up and said: "You'll do me, I'll *have* you." There was nowhere to run, no where to go, and only two shots left in the rifle.

Luke and the others were about quarter of a mile away; the country's so flat they could see what was going on, but were too far off to do anything. Just sat on their horses and watched. Big Rupert said to Luke: "I think he's going to bore him, that feller. Bin bore him up that feller quick now."

Anyway, the bull came at me, and I hit him with the next shot, spun him round and he went down. Before he could get up again I trotted up and fired my last shot into his head.

But it had been rather a close call, simply because I was feeling pretty weak.

I went back to the others and Luke said: "How'd you go?"

I said: "Ah, I muffed it."

"Yair," said Luke, "we thought he was going to have you for a bit." So did I.

To survive everything else, get rescued, and then get clobbered by a bull out on the flat would have been a bit hard.

We camped that night at a place they called the Brook, a nice freshwater creek. Virtually no trees about, but plenty of good grass for the horses. Very good camp.

As we'd been going along I'd had places pointed out to me, in the distance, which are sacred areas, and away to our right from the Brook, there was an Aboriginal burial spot, where the body had been put up in a tree. The ranges on the boundary they called High Lonesome. These are all whitefellow names, but they have blackfellow or old-time names for the same places, which I'm afraid I don't remember properly, and wouldn't spell right either, most likely.

The next day, I walked a good deal of the way across the floor of the Valley. In some ways it was better than riding bareback, and it gave the horse a bit of a rest. Everyone else changed horses every day, but I rode the same one, old Cooney, the whole time. Not many average stockhorses are cooperative about people hopping on them bareback.

The dogs and the horses had got used to each other, got on well by now, and the pups were running along under the horses' bellies during the heat of the day, to keep in the shade. The horses just kept walking along, took no notice. Cindy was still on three legs, but going real well.

Down toward the far end of the Valley a mob of brumbies came trotting out over the plain to have a look at us, curious. Stopped to have a look, sniff the air and snort, then wheel away again, long manes and tails streaming as they went. Their run seemed to be from the Brook to our next camp, at Lonely Springs near the foot of more hills.

Rupert, Raphael, and Christopher cooked the rib bones from our killer that night, Aboriginal style, wrapped up in paper bark from trees near the creek. It was very good too, but I was feeling too sick again to eat much at all. Very woozy, and throwing up again.

Luke and the others went into a bit of a huddle, talking things over. I knew they were wondering if I was going to finish the ride, make it to Palumpa. Luke told me later that they thought about leaving me camped with one bloke while the others went on to the station and sent for a helicopter to come out and pick me up, then decided that wasn't feasible, so reckoned they would just have to tie me to my horse if I got too crook. Personally, I never thought I was going to get as sick as that, and am just as pleased that the bit about tying me to the horse wasn't necessary. Not the nicest way to travel. It's funny, but the riding back, the getting out of the Fitzmaurice, was in some ways harder than it had been staying there.

It was a steep climb up a big hill the next morning, and then across to another jump-up, going down this time. And very steep. Raphael lost the trail at one point, took a while to pick up the pad again, and we were all stuck there, halfway down this bloody cliff.

"No way down unless we fly," Luke reckoned. "We're angels, but we're not that good."

Raphael got it all sorted out, and we moved on again. Then Christopher said a few words, absolutely deadpan: "The pack's slipped off the horse." It had too. One of the packs had come off right over the packhorse's head. It was steep all right, down that last big jump-up.

It was still a bit rough when we got to the bottom, but by the time we camped that night, the fifth since leaving the Fitzmaurice, at Mocumba, one of their old stockcamps, near an enormous boab tree, we were out on the big, black soil Palumpa plain. And would get to the homestead the next day.

The whole trip—or expedition, you could call it—from Palumpa out to the Fitzmaurice, and then back again, was as good an example as you could wish to see of Aboriginal bushcraft. A lot of it was over very rough bad country with a general scarcity of water holes. Raphael hadn't been over the Old Blackfellow Trail for well over thirty years, but he knew the way and could find the water holes. The same applied to Big Rupert.

We were so absolutely on course that, out in the Valley, we came on to an old tree which had been chopped down for honey, a wild bees' nest, years and years ago. "That's right," they said. "Old man come up here long time ago, very long time. Came this way. Got honey here." They're good bushmen, no doubt about that. No maps, only the picture of the country in their minds, a memory which hadn't been refreshed for a long time. But they knew it. No worries at all.

They also had their own idea about what had caused my

accident in the first place. What had overturned my boat. Luke told me that they said it was the Rainbow Snake. According to Aboriginal legends, the Rainbow Snake lives in rivers and estuaries, and sometimes turns boats and things over; doesn't attack anyone, just gets them dumped in the water. I suppose you could say it has a funny sense of humor.

Well, the Rainbow Snake is as good an explanation as any, because I still don't know what did it.

4

The Road Home

We rode past the station airstrip: as a symbol of civilization it was a more acceptable one than the empty oil drum floating up the Fitzmaurice.

Another mile or so of track winding through fairly thick timber, past a notice which said something along the lines of: "Visitors please only leave footprints behind." Very good. A gate. And—Palumpa. A scattered group of neat-looking buildings beyond a big billabong crammed with water birds. That billabong with its bird life is one of Palumpa's pride and joys. Bells and hobble chains jingling, the horses strung out past some houses; a couple of kids waved, jumped up and down and ran inside, no doubt to tell their mums. A generator thumped a steady beat, the horses swung past a big shed—workshop and garage—and we pulled up near Luke's house.

We dismounted. The horses sighed and shook their heads, pretty glad to be home. The generator kept thumping away. It was all a bit strange, hard to take in, after the Fitzmaurice. Up till now we had still been out in the bush. Sure, I was with other men and horses, but we were still out in the bush.

Now houses. With lawns. And white painted fences round
them. That generator thumping like a giant heartbeat. And
people, starting to come from here and there. And getting excited. Asking questions. All curious. "Where'd they capture that
whitefeller, eh? Where'd he come from?"

Well, I must have been unexpected, that's for sure, but I
didn't feel like saying much. Let Luke and the others do most
of the talking.

I was back. In civilization again. It was good, but it was still
a bit hard to adjust to it, at first. Sitting on Luke's veranda,
fly wire all round, clean floor, no dust, no flies. Cool and comfortable, but a bit strange. There was a white family there, on
Palumpa, as well as Luke. The Hupfields. Richard was the
mechanic and Caroline the bookkeeper, and Caroline took me
over to their house for a feed.

Fried rice. That was the first meal I'd had sitting at a table
for a long time. A table with a shiny top, with a china plate
and knives and forks and tea out of a cup with a saucer.
Everything seemed sort of emphasized, accentuated. The white
china, the bright colors in the curtains, the shiny surfaces of
things. Noises sounded different, too. A kettle whistling was
so loud. Clatter of kitchen things. Creak of a fly-wire door.
The cockatoos screeching outside in the hot sun were in another world. But to see a woman and children again, that was
really getting back to everyday life. It was good. I didn't even
mind the kids playing with my dogs, making a fuss of them,
spoiling them a bit.

To most people a place like Palumpa would seem very isolated, lonely. But if you came into it from being out somewhere like the Fitzmaurice it would seem a pretty big sort of
a turnout. And you'd be very aware of all the things that have
come to mean civilization in these days. Electricity. Being able
to turn a switch and get light. A bathroom with hot water. A

mirror to shave by—so that's who I was: "That's me, that bloke there in the mirror." A radio playing music—pop tunes. The news—all the trials and troubles, gossip and confusion out there in the rest of the world, all coming out of that little machine. And a bed to sleep in that night.

Palumpa's a good place, very well run. The cattle numbers aren't all that great yet, it is not the best cattle country you could wish for, but they do supply a lot of the meat for Port Keats, over on the coast, which is a pretty big settlement. If they can find a way to use the good country, like in the Majallindi Valley and around Cooliman Creek, then the cattle side of the station will go ahead. But in the meantime, as an Aboriginal community project, it's very good. Everything is clean, tidy, well looked after. The Aboriginal Council makes the decisions about what they want, and Luke sees that they're carried out. He and Big Rupert and the rest of the Council have a very good understanding and relationship, so everything runs smoothly.

There's no grog allowed on Palumpa at all. No exceptions. If somebody is so foolish as to arrive on Palumpa with booze under his arm he gets flattened by Luke. Gets told off afterward, but flattened first. It isn't very often necessary. People know that's the rule, which is the decision of the Council. And anyone who has seen the damage grog has done, and is still doing, to Aboriginal communities all over the country, knows why the Council has banned it on Palumpa.

I enjoyed being there, seeing the place, and how it was run, but I had to get back to Kununurra and try to pick up some sort of normal routine again, so a charter plane was booked from Darwin to come and pick me up.

That saw another bit of a hitch, or almost. The charter pilot didn't know anything about what had happened. He'd just got this job to pick up a bloke from Palumpa and take him to Kununurra. And he didn't want to take the dogs. There was no way I'd leave them behind and I didn't feel like explaining things. So things got a bit heated, and I eventually offered to sort it all out down on the flat if he'd just step down from his plane for a minute. I suppose you could say I lost my temper. Anyway, the dogs came with me.

And on the way back we flew right over the Fitzmaurice. I could look down on where my old camp was. A slightly different view to the one I'd had for the past seven weeks or so. Made you think a bit.

Kununurra. The red hills, the green water of the Diversion Dam. It looked a pretty good spot. The little airport, and . . . a walk into town. No one knew I was coming back that day, so there was no one to meet me. I didn't mind, I hadn't expected anything different. And it wasn't a long walk. The last lap home, shouldering the swag with the two puppy dogs trotting along behind. Not quite all the way, I got a lift in a truck for the last few hundred yards. The driver didn't ask any questions and I didn't say where I'd been.

And when I saw Lorraine, she just said: "I thought you should've got back about now. How'd it go? Where've you been?"

There's a song by Ted Egan (a bush singer, very popular up here) called, "I've been around a bit, said the man from Humpty Doo." Because of the way I'm always inclined to just shove off for a few days or weeks without saying much about where I'm going, it'd become a bit of a joke. If I was asked where I'd been, I'd just say: "Ah, I've been around a bit."

I'd got back, was still in one piece, I was all right. So that's all I said: "I've been around a bit."

Postscript

I didn't tell anyone, not even Lorraine, what had happened. Not at first. When I'd been back a bit, routine was once more flowing smooth, I felt better, and had been out to retrieve my vehicle from the bank of the Victoria River, then I did tell her that I'd been stranded out there for about two months. Told her just a bit about it, and she said: "Just as well your parents didn't find out or they'd have a fit." Little did I know that it was going to be all over the newspapers and they did have a fit.

I hadn't talked about it because I really didn't think it all that important. What I'd lost was a couple of months and what I'd gained was some experience. I just wanted the whole thing kept quiet, no fuss. Maybe I shouldn't have got stranded in the first place, but these things happen. It's like riding horses—you shouldn't fall off, but on occasion you do.

There was also the fact that, in truth, I shouldn't, not really, have been anywhere near where I was. Heading into an area near an Aboriginal reserve, which is out of bounds. I shouldn't have had my vehicle on station country without permission.

There's a lot of things which don't matter unless something goes wrong, and then they do matter because people find out and may take exception.

And there was my family. Especially my parents. All parents worry, that's more or less a parent's lot, so what they didn't know wasn't going to worry them. I could see no point in saying: "Oh, by the way, Mum, I got stranded out in the bush for a couple of months." No point at all. A bit like yelling, "Fire!" after the house has burned down.

The people at Palumpa had said they'd keep the story quiet, but apparently someone at Port Keats heard about it, and from there it got to the newspapers. As far as I was concerned everything was just going along quietly and then, all of a sudden, Bang! There's headlines in the Darwin *Star* weeks after it had all happened. Which caused all sorts of confusion because the paper had got the times all arse about face and it read like it had just happened the day before. So people said, "Rubbish!" because they'd seen me around town for the past three weeks or so. "That's not right. Can't be right," they said. "Saw him last week," sort of thing. The story even had phrases like, "Mr. Ansell said . . . 'in this country you either learn quick or die young,'" which I probably had said, but not to the newspaper. I was a bit upset about it all and rang the Darwin office and more or less abused them, and they apologized and were sorry they'd caused me trouble. But there it was. Done. What I also didn't know then was that the story was going to be picked up by every paper all over the country.

Then there was the poetry thing. That was another thing I'd never told people I did, write poetry. Not even my mates knew until it was printed in the paper that I did, and their reaction was: "Get away! You're having me on!" And when I said that it was true, they looked at me a bit askance. I didn't really mind, but it was something that up till then I'd always kept to myself. I'd recite poems, bush poems, that they all knew and liked: "Johnson's Snakebite Antidote," things that you'd get a laugh at, recite them all night, if you wanted. But to actually make up poems myself, well, no one knew that.

One thing is that most bushmen are very private people, all the time, always are. But if you're going to write a poem and put anything in it, that can only come from yourself. You've got to put yourself there, and you don't want to put that up for display in general. It was just something I'd done for my own interest, that's all. And hadn't at all thought about publishing it. For one thing it's not modern poetry, which to me is a Chinese jigsaw puzzle with a difference, a lot of abstract thoughts put down on paper and the whole object is a guessing game: "What's he thinking? What's he trying to say?" Maybe I've a funny idea about poetry, but it seems to me that if you can't put your message so someone can understand it, as clearly and concisely as you can, and so that it sounds nice, then it isn't poetry.

Anyway, that was out of the bag. Writing poetry. And so was the Fitzmaurice story. A few people were very skeptical about the whole thing, some probably still are, but I can't help that. People who knew me asked if it was true, and when I said it was, they said: "Why didn't you say something?" But I just hadn't wanted to at the time. I'd come out of it all right. That was the end of it. You don't bother mentioning things that might have happened. I don't know why it is, but it's part of the code of the country, or something. Everyone plays it cool, and after a while it's not "playing it cool," it becomes— something else. I don't know quite how to put it.

All the blokes up in this country, blokes who work with cattle, ringers, stockmen, bull catchers, whatever, all of them, have really narrow shaves all the time. But they never talk about it. If they do it's always underplayed in a big way. For example,

I know a bloke who got horned by one of the biggest bulls ever, got opened right up, and nearly died. You can stick pins in his stomach where all the plastic surgery was done. But, if the subject comes up, if he mentions it at all, the only thing he'll say is: "Ah, had a bit of trouble with a mickey once. Put a little hole in me."

I think the opinion is that if you come through in one piece, and you're still alive, then nothing else really matters. The event is over. Maybe it goes deeper than that. Like stock-camp life itself. The life of the ringers. Where they sleep on the ground and eat shocking tucker, and yet it's all right. They wouldn't think of complaining. Work seven days a week and get mongrel horses to ride, but that's all right. If you complain, you'd be known as a whinger and of no value to the country. If you can't hack the pace you've got to get out. That's how the ringer looks at things—the bull catchers and all of them. And they all do work which has an element of danger, do it all the time. It's accepted, is a part of it.

So, looking at it like that, what was so special about getting stuck up on the Fitzmaurice? What I'd been through was relatively minor. I didn't even get a bone broken. And I've spent plenty of time in hospital from rolling the catcher or having old scrub bulls jumping on me, that kind of thing. As far as I was concerned it could have been bad, real bad, the ultimate yarn where you don't come through. But it wasn't. It turned out all right.

It's like going out to shoot a kangaroo. You don't come back and say you missed him by an inch. You either got him or you didn't.

So that is how I looked at it all. Until the papers got hold of the story, and that changed a lot of things.

The next day I got a phone call from Richard Oxenburgh Productions asking for the exclusive film and TV rights to the

whole thing, and I agreed to that. Which might sound a bit of
an about-turn, but the damage was done as far as keeping quiet
went, so I thought, "What the hell, why not?" and agreed.
There was a monetary consideration, too. I'd been sitting
on the Fitzmaurice, not working and with contracts being
dishonored and things like that, so I was in a bit of financial
difficulty. I had never considered the thing, the adventure or
whatever you like to call it, was worth money, but now that
it was I was quite glad to get something for it. At that stage,
too, it was virtually money for nothing, because it was just for
the exclusive rights with only the possibility that the film would
actually go ahead. Then when everyone else did want to go
ahead with it that was okay because I had agreed to do it. And
I was interested to see what went on, as I didn't know anything about the film industry, so it was a new experience. And
maybe some of the mistakes made in the newspaper story could
be cleared up, even little things like the paper saying I was a
buffalo shooter, which was wrong. Bull catching is an entirely
different game.

Clearing up that point was easy enough, about the only thing
that was, as it turned out. I didn't know what I was letting
myself in for, that's for sure. Neither did the filmmakers, when
it comes to that. But one thing the producers and I were dead
set agreed on was that we wanted it authentic. Didn't want to
put anything in—or take anything out, either—just to make it
look nicer, or more glamorous, or something.

We worked bloody hard to get it as right as we possibly
could. Everyone did. Even Luke McCall, Big Rupert, and old
Raphael rode all the way across from Palumpa with their string
of horses to meet up with us at the Fitzmaurice. Just as it had
happened. Except Christopher didn't come. He had shot off
to Bathurst Island or somewhere, so that meant the first
change—three for the "rescue scene" instead of four.

Then a monstrous great bushfire came in from miles away, right across the ranges, right onto the river. Burned out all the far side. That head-high cane grass went off like a rocket. Luke and the blackfellows had to shift pretty smartly to save their gear and horses, being camped on that side. There was no way the camera could ignore all that burned-out country, so we had to film the fire to explain it, although there wasn't any bushfire the first time I was there.

There were quite a lot of things which were different. Even the dogs, sort of. Bouncer was a pretty grown-up dog by then. And Cindy had gone over to Queensland, so old Deaf Dog came along instead. Trouble was, he fought with Bouncer. Terrible for continuity. Old Deaf Dog is white, and every scratch on his nose showed up.

Transport was a real headache. I got my old catching vehicle and another Toyota all the way into the river, and a truck part of the way, but the film crew and all their gear had to go in by helicopter.

But the biggest problem, of course, was the country itself. The fact that, up there, the country is boss, and doesn't give a damn about schedules or budgets or plans in general. As I've said before, you can't push it. So the film didn't quite turn out as planned. All the same, I reckon it does show what it's like there, on the Fitzmaurice, or anywhere in the Top End that's still wild country. And gives some idea of what it's like to be stuck there on your own. Which is what the whole thing was all about.

One thing I was aware of. Making the film wasn't going to do me much good up here in the North. Proving the point about the story being true or not wouldn't matter that much. Because the people it would affect, who affect me, are the people who live where I work, and know me. And people up here, for some reason, have a phobia about appearing on the media.

So that would be detrimental to my standing in their eyes. No matter what. Whether I proved it was the Greatest Survival Story of All Time or whether I proved it was not. That is irrelevant to the fact that I got up in front of a camera and that is a terrible thing to do.

But, I had agreed to do it, and it was a very interesting experience, no doubt about that. I don't regret having done it. From there we have gone on to this book, and that includes some of the poems.

I suppose, looking at it all, that once the first story appeared in the newspaper headlines, that was it. No point in trying to keep any sort of low profile after that, and no point in going in for half measures either. One thing is for sure, the repercussions from a casually planned fishing trip have gone on for a very long time, and another thing: salt water has lost any fascination it ever held for me. The sea just isn't my line of country at all.